Sample Exam Q

ISTQB

Foundation Level-Agile Tester Extension Exam
(CTFL-AT)

Chhavi Raj Dosaj

ISTQB certified registered trainer for ISTQB Foundation Level
(CTFL) & ISTQB Foundation Level- Agile Tester Extension
(CTFL-AT)

Sample Exam Questions - ISTQB Foundation Level-Agile Tester Extension Exam (CTFL-AT)

© 2016 AdactIn Group Pty Ltd

ISBN-13: 978-1533567420

Published by
AdactIn Group Pty Ltd

Contents

About the Author

C. Raj Dosaj,
B.E (Computer Technology),CTFL,CTFL-AT

C. Raj Dosaj has more than 15 years of experience in functional Testing and analysis of Banking, Investment banking, and credit systems/platforms for large financial services companies in diverse geographies like; Australia, India, Hong Kong, Europe and the US.

He started his career with TCS and worked on various technical consulting projects for a wide range of global clients like American Express, Lehman Brothers, Macquarie Securities, Daiwa Securities, Deutsche Bank, London Clearing House, Westpac, Commonwealth Bank and many more. He is currently working with Reserve Bank of Australia in Sydney.

He is an ISTQB certified registered trainer for ISTQB Foundation Level (CTFL) and ISTQB Foundation Level- Agile Tester Extension (CTFL-AT) certifications. As an experienced corporate trainer, he has trained professionals for Cubic Transportation System Sydney, Credit Union Australia and other Adactin group corporate clients.

He holds a Bachelor's Degree in Computer Technology from Nagpur University, India.

Preface

I wrote this book with the following three categories of readers in mind:

The first category is of people who are planning to take the exam in the near future. They should go through the syllabus in chapter 1, research the topic and then attempt the sample exams to check their understanding about the subject. The sample exams can be used to find the areas of strength and weakness confidence.

The second category is of people who are working in Agile projects and want to test their knowledge of Agile Testing based on the ISTQB syllabus.

The third category is of teachers who can use these sample papers to measure their students' understanding of each syllabus chapter by focusing on specific questions from that particular chapter.

These sample exams can also be used as an aid to passing the exam with minimal effort

Disclaimer:

Although all efforts have been made to ensure the accuracy of the contents of this book, we cannot guarantee 100% correctness of the information contained herein.

If you find any factual anomalies, grammar or spelling errors please send it along with your comments and suggestions to the author. Good luck on the exam questions!

Acknowledgements

I would like to acknowledge that this book relies heavily on the ISTQB-Agile Tester Extension Syllabus and Standard Glossary of Terms used in Software Testing. In some cases, certain phrases were used verbatim to ensure the content adheres to the syllabus and glossary.

I would like to thank my parents Dr Pradeep Dosaj and Kaushal Dosaj for their unconditional support and for allowing me to realize my own potential, my wife Shikha for her continuous support without which this book would not have been possible.

Special thanks to my dear friend Richard Clifton for helping in the technical review of this book.

I would also like to thank my friends Sapna Bhatia and Navneesh Garg who always inspire me to take new challenges every day.

Feedback and Queries

For any feedback or queries you can contact the author at www.adactin.com/contact.html or email chhavi.raj@adactin.com

Order this book

For bulk orders, contact us at orders@adactin.com

You can also place your order online at adactin.com/store/

1. Overview of Exam

Introduction to Foundation Level Agile Tester Extension

The certification for Foundation Level Extension – Agile Tester is designed for professionals who are working within Agile environments. It is also for professionals who are planning to start implementing Agile methods in the near future, or are working within companies that plan to do so. The certification provides an advantage for those who would like to know the required Agile activities, roles, methods, and methodologies specific to their role.

Intended Audience

The Foundation Level Extension – Agile Tester qualification is aimed at four groups of professionals:

1. Professionals who have achieved in-depth testing experience in traditional methods and would like to get an Agile Tester Certificate.

2. Junior professional testers who are just starting in the testing profession, have received the Foundation Level certificate, and would like to know more about the tester's role in an Agile environment.

3. Professionals who are relatively new to testing and are required to implement test approaches, methods and techniques in their day to day job in Agile projects.

4. Professionals who are experienced in their role (including unit testing) and need more understanding and knowledge about how to perform and manage testing on all levels in Agile projects.

These professionals include people who are in roles such as testers, test analysts, test engineers, test consultants, test managers, user acceptance testers, and software developers.

This Foundation Level Extension – Agile Tester certification may also be appropriate for anyone who wants a deeper understanding of software testing in the Agile world, such as project managers, quality managers, software development managers, business analysts, IT directors, and management consultants.

Career Paths for Testers

Building on the Foundation Level, the Agile Tester Extension supports the definition of career paths for professional testers. A person with the Agile Tester certificate has extended the broad understanding of testing acquired at the Foundation Level to enable him or her to work effectively as a professional tester in an Agile project. People possessing an ISTQB Foundation Level Extension – Agile Tester certificate may use the Certified Tester Foundation Level acronym CTFL-AT.

Learning Objectives

The syllabus categorizes learning objectives into three cognitive levels:

- **K1:** remember, recognize, and recall

- **K2:** understand, explain, give reasons, compare, classify and summarize

- **K3:** apply

The relevant learning objectives at K1, K2, and K3 levels are provided at the beginning of each chapter within each particular extension syllabus.

Entry Requirements

To be able to participate in a Foundation Level Extension – Agile Tester exam, candidates must have obtained the ISTQB Foundation Level certificate.

Agile Tester Extension Exam Structure

Similar to the Foundation Level Certification exam, the Agile Tester Certification exam is comprised of 40 multiple choice questions, with a pass mark of 65% to be completed within 60 minutes.

Overview of the Foundation Level Extension – Agile Tester Syllabus

Business Outcomes

This section lists the Business Outcomes expected of a candidate who has achieved the Foundation Level Extension – Agile Tester certification. An Agile Tester can...

AFM1 Collaborate in a cross-functional Agile team being familiar with principles and basic practices of Agile software development.

AFM2 Adapt existing testing experience and knowledge to Agile values and principles.

AFM3 Support the Agile team in planning test-related activities.

AFM4 Apply relevant methods and techniques for testing in an Agile project.

AFM5 Assist the Agile team in test automation activities.

AFM6 Assist business stakeholders in defining understandable and testable user stories, scenarios, requirements and acceptance criteria as appropriate.

AFM7 Work and share information with other team members using effective communication styles and channels.

In general, a Certified Tester Foundation Level – Agile Tester is expected to have acquired the necessary skills to work effectively within an Agile team and environment.

Content

Chapter 1: Agile Software Development

- The tester should remember the basic concept of Agile software development based on the Agile Manifesto.

- The tester should understand the advantages of the whole-team approach and the benefits of early and frequent feedback.

- The tester should recall Agile software development approaches.

- The tester should be able to write testable user stories in collaboration with developers and business representatives.

- The tester should understand how retrospectives can be used as a mechanism for process improvement in Agile projects.

- The tester should understand the use and purpose of continuous integration.

- The tester should know the differences between iteration and release planning, and how a tester adds value in each of these activities.

Chapter 2: Fundamental Agile Testing Principles, Practices, and Processes

- The tester should be able to describe the differences between testing activities in Agile projects and non-Agile projects.

- The tester should be able to describe how development and testing activities are integrated in Agile projects.

- The tester should be able to describe the role of independent testing in Agile projects.

- The tester should be able to describe the tools and techniques used to communicate the status of testing in an Agile project, including test progress and product quality.

- The tester should be able to describe the process of evolving tests across multiple iterations and explain why test automation is important to manage regression risk in Agile projects.

- The tester should understand the skills (people, domain, and testing) of a tester in an Agile team.

- The tester should be able to understand the role of a tester within an Agile team.

Chapter 3: Agile Testing Methods, Techniques, and Tools

- The tester should be able to recall the concepts of test-driven development, acceptance test driven development, and behavior-driven development.

- The tester should be able to recall the concepts of the test pyramid.

- The tester should be able to summarize the testing quadrants and their relationships with testing levels and testing types.

- For a given Agile project, the tester should be able to work as a tester in a Scrum team.

- The tester should be able to assess quality risks within an Agile project.

- The tester should be able to estimate testing effort based on iteration content and quality risks.

- The tester should be able to interpret relevant information to support testing activities.

- The tester should be able to explain to business stakeholders how to define testable acceptance criteria.

- Given a user story, the tester should be able to write acceptance test-driven development test cases.

- For both functional and non-functional behavior, the tester should be able to write test cases using black box test design techniques based on given user stories.

- The tester should be able to perform exploratory testing to support the testing of an Agile project.

- The tester should be able to recall different tools available to testers according to their purpose and to activities in Agile projects.

Trademarks

The following registered trademarks and service marks are used in this document: ISTQB® is a registered trademark of the International Software Testing Qualifications Board

2. Agile Tester Extension Sample Exam 1

Question 1

Which of the following is NOT an Agile Manifesto statement of values?

Answer:

A. Customer collaboration over contract negotiation

B. Responding to change over following a plan

C. Processes and tools over individuals and interactions

D. Working software over comprehensive documentation

Question 2

Which of the following statement best reflects one of the values of the Agile Manifesto?

Answer:

A. Responding to change allows an Agile team to develop relevant, helpful product that people want to use.

B. The team should try to automate all unit test cases to reduce regression testing effort.

C. Business representatives should participate in all project activities.

D. Testers should work collaboratively with Business and developer team.

Question 3

Who is responsible for the quality of the product in Agile projects?

Answer:

A. Testers as they are testing the product before it reaches the real customer

B. Developers as they are developing the product based on the requirements

C. Business Analyst as they are responsible for writing the acceptance criteria for the product

D. The whole Team has responsibility for the quality of the product

E. The Product owner as they specifies the customer requirements to the team.

Question 4

Which of the following can be used to take advantage of the whole team approach in Agile development?

Answer:

A. Daily stand-up meeting

B. Continuous integration

C. Test Driven Development

D. Pairing

Question 5

Which TWO of the following statements are true?

1. Early feedback can only be achieved by Continuous Integration

2. Early and frequent feedback helps manage the team better since the capability of the team is transparent to everyone.

3. Early and frequent feedback helps the team find the high severity bugs early.

4. Early and frequent feedback enables an agile team to build a product which reflects what the customer wants.

Answer:

A. 1 and 4

B. 2 and 3

C. 2 and 4

D. 1 and 3

Question 6

Which of the following is NOT a benefit of early feedback?

A. Avoiding requirements misunderstandings

B. Clarifying customers requests, making them available for customer use early

C. Early discovery and resolution of bugs

D. Early feedback reduces costs because it decreases the amount of time needed for testing.

Question 7

Which of the following is NOT one of the values to guide development in Extreme Programming?

Answer:

A. Simplicity

B. Quality

C. Courage

D. Feedback

E. Communication

Question 8

During an iteration planning meeting, the team is discussing a user story. The product owner advises that sensitive customer data is captured as part of the story and should be encrypted. The developer explains that the encryption could result in an increase in development time.

Which of the following would best represent a tester's contribution to this discussion?

Answer:

A. The tester advises that encryption will increase the testing effort as there is more development required.

B. The tester advises that the priority of the story should be increased.

C. The tester advises that more performance testing will be required for the user story.

D. The tester advises that the user story needs testable acceptance criteria for the encryption functionality.

Question 9

Which of the following BEST describes a tester's contribution in a retrospective meeting?

Answer:

A. As a tester participating in a retrospective meeting, I should only be concerned about the test-related improvement decisions focused on test effectiveness

B. As a tester, I should I should give feedback only on the automation tasks so that I can improve test effectiveness

C. As a tester, I should provide feedback on all activities conducted by the agile team during all the completed sprints.

D. As a tester, I should give feedback only on the development task so that I can improve test effectiveness

Question 10

Which of the following could be raised in the retrospective meeting?

Answer:

i. Frequent Environment related issues are slowing down testing. A root cause analysis of the environment issues is required.

ii. A new tool is needed for the team to better manage user stories.

iii. Automation coverage of unit tests should be increased to improve overall quality

iv. The team should plan for some social activity after the end of each iteration

Answer:

A. i, ii, iii

B. i and iii

C. i, ii, iv

D. i, ii, iii, iv

Question 11

Which TWO of the following are benefits of Continuous Integration?

1. It allows earlier detection and easier root cause analysis of integration problems and conflicting changes.
2. It gives the development team regular feedback on whether the code is working
3. Eliminate the need for a System test after the new changes are introduced.
4. The code check in process is fast with continuous integration

Answer:

A. 1 and 4
B. 1 and 2
C. 2 and 4
D. 1 and 3

Question 12

Which of the following TWO activities will the tester be involved in during iteration planning?

1. Discuss the Test approach and test plan with the Team
2. Help break down user stories into smaller and more detailed tasks
3. Estimate testing tasks generated by new features planned for this iteration.
4. Support the clarification of the user stories and ensure that they are testable

Answer:

A. 1 and 4
B. 2 and 3
C. 2 and 4
D. 1 and 3

Question 13

Which of the following is NOT related to a 'User Story'?

Answer:

A. Story Acceptance criteria.

B. Story point.

C. Story priority.

D. Story Entry criteria.

Question 14

Which of the following test activities is typically done during agile projects, but is not as common on traditional projects?

Answer:

A. Testers prepare detailed test strategy to address all testing activities during each iteration.

B. Testers spend a lot of time creating, executing and maintaining automated tests and results.

C. Testers use defect based techniques to find defects.

D. Testers used risk based testing as one of the test strategies.

Question 15

Consider the following work products used by Agile team for development and testing activities:

i.   Quality risk catalogs

ii.   Test Results log

iii. User stories

iv.   automated unit tests

which of the above are Test work products ?

Answer:

A.   i and ii

B.   ii only

C.   i and iii

D.   All of the above.

Question 16

The Test manager wants to introduce Independent testing for one of the Agile teams. Which of the following is a good approach?

Answer:

A.   Engage the independent test team in iteration planning activities

B.   Engage the independent test team during the release planning to understand the risk

C.   Engage the independent team carrying out test levels that might not fit well within a sprint

D.   Engage the independent test team for the automation tasks during the sprints

Question 17

Which TWO of the following statements are true for independent test teams on agile projects?

Answer:

1. Independent test Teams can be used for creating and supporting test environments and data.

2. Independent testers can work on all the iteration testing activities.

3. Independent test teams can work as 'on demand' testers during the final days of each sprint..

4. Independent testers can work on all the iteration automation activities.

Answer:

A. 1 and 4

B. 1 and 2

C. 2 and 4

D. 1 and 3

Question 18

What is the best way to measure the Agile team's progress against the estimates?

Answer:

A. Test Status reports

B. Burndown charts

C. Number of completed stories in the sprint

D. Test Summary report

Question 19

During the final days of sprint tests, execution is blocked due to a test environment related issue which is escalated to the environment team. What is the BEST action point from a Tester's point of view?

Answer:

A. There is nothing the tester can do so he should start working on test case preparation for stories which can be included in the next sprint.

B. This is a blocker and should be communicated in the daily stand-up meeting so the team can help resolve the issue or look for alternative solutions to finish testing.

C. Environment downtime can be used effectively to work on the automation of test cases.

D. The tester should document this so it can be raised in the retrospective as this may impact the testing for the current sprint.

Question 20

The Agile team has created an automation acceptance test suit to manage regression risk due to frequent changes in the project. This is now part of the continuous integration full system build, what should be the frequency of run?

Answer:

A. Daily

B. Weekly

C. Each code check

D. At least once in the sprint

Question 21

Which of the following can be used to reduce regression risk due to high code churn in Agile projects?

Answer:

A. Automation done for test data generation

B. Automation done for unit tests

C. Automation done to compare data outputs

D. Automation done to restore test environment to baseline

Question 22

Which of the following are necessary skills for a Tester working on agile projects?

i.   Competent in test automation

ii.   Competent in alpha/ beta testing

iii. Competent in experience-based testing

iv.   Competent in unit testing

Answer:

A. i, ii and iii

B. i, ii, iii and iv

C. i and iii

D. i, iii and iv

Question 23

Which tasks are typically expected of a tester within an Agile team?

i.   Decide on user acceptance

ii.   Understanding, implementing, and updating the test strategy

iii. Prepare burndown charts

iv.   Configuring, using, and managing test environments and test data

v.   Decide on priority of the user story

Answer:

A.   i and iii

B.   ii and iii

C.   ii &iv

D.   ii & v

Question 24

Which of the following is NOT a test related organization risk which Agile organizations may encounter?

Answer:

A.   Testers work so closely to developers that they lose the appropriate tester mindset

B.   Testers become tolerant about inefficient, ineffective, or low-quality practices within the team

C.   Testers cannot keep pace with the incoming changes in time-constrained iterations

D.   Testers spend more time on Automation related activities rather than on testing.

Question 25

The term "velocity" refers to which of the following?

Answer:

A. A Velocity chart shows the sum of estimates of the work delivered across iterations; this may be used while selecting the stories for the next iteration

B. A Velocity chart shows the degree to which the source code of a program is tested by a particular test. This may be used to show the code coverage

C. A Velocity chart shows the count of number of defects discovered during a given period. This may be used as criteria for stopping the testing.

D. A Velocity chart shows the number of source code changes per iteration; this may be used to know the code coverage

Question 26

Which of the following statements about Behavior-Driven Development (BDD) is FALSE?

Answer:

A. BDD allows a developer to focus on testing the code based on the expected behavior of the software.

B. BDD allows the developer to collaborate with other stakeholders, including testers, to define accurate unit tests focused on business needs.

C. In BDD, automated test cases are created before coding starts.

D. The result of BDD is test classes used by the developer to develop test cases

Question 27

The foundation layer of the 'Test Pyramid' is made up of which tests?

Answer:

A. Unit/component tests

B. System level tests.

C. Integration level tests

D. Acceptance level tests

Question 28

In the release planning session the tester is communicating the test ideas using testing quadrants so that the team understands the purpose of all the test types and test levels included in the development lifecycle.

Which of the following tester statements about testing quadrants is true?

Answer:

A. Quadrant Q1 are unit level tests and Quadrant Q4 are functional tests.

B. Quadrant Q1 are unit level tests and Quadrant Q4 are user acceptance tests.

C. Quadrant Q3 are performance tests and Quadrant Q4 are functional tests.

D. Quadrant Q2 are functional tests and Quadrant Q4 are performance tests.

Question 29

Given the following user story:

"As a bank customer, I can easily view my bank statements for the last 5 years"

"For all customers, the system must display all queries in less than 4 seconds, 90% of the time"

And the associated test cases:

Test Case 1: Login as bank customer. Verify that the customer transaction history is available for the last 5 years.

Test Case 2: Verify in a realistic environment that the customer can view the statement in less than 4 seconds.

Which TWO test quadrants would the above test cases be part of?

Answer:

A.   Q1 unit level, technology facing & Q2 system level, business facing

B.   Q2 system level, business facing & Q3 system or user acceptance level, business facing

C.   Q1 unit level, technology facing & Q4 system or operation acceptance level, technology facing

D.   Q2 system level, business facing & Q4 system or operation acceptance level, technology facing

Question 30

There is a new feature in scope for the current sprint which will results in changes to the existing database tables. The testers on the team realize that this change can introduce bugs and it may require major changes in the existing scripts and the automation framework.

What is the best course of action for the testers to take?

Answer:

A.   The testers will calculate the extra time required and update the team that they have to work extra hours in order to update the existing test scripts and automation framework during the existing sprint plan.

B.   The testers will notify the team of the issue. A risk analysis is done and the team decides what regression testing must be performed to find the defects introduced by the new changes. The testers will update the sprint plan by adding tasks to modify the framework and scripts to support the new changes.

C.   The current testing tasks need to be completed for the sprint. The testers continue with their existing sprint plan and make no changes to the test automation framework or scripts.

D.   The testers will stop what they are doing and start working on the automation framework & script modifications and communicate with the team that any other testing work for the sprint will have to be pushed to the next iteration.

Question 31

An Agile team is doing the quality risk analysis for three user stories selected from the backlog during an iteration planning session. Match the stories with their respective quality risk based on the information below:

User Story 1: Program to calculate the account interest information for the financial end of year report.

User Story 2: Program to store the customer sensitive information.

User Story 3: A front end screen for the system used by senior citizens.

Answer:

A.   User Story 1 : Security ,User Story 2: Functional ,User Story 3: Usability

B.   User Story 1 : Functional ,User Story 2: Security ,User Story 3: Usability

C.   User Story 1 : Usability, User Story 2: Security, User Story 3: Functional

D.   User Story 1 : Functional, User Story 2: Usability, User Story 3: Security

Question 32

During the poker planning session, the following story points were given to a particular user story

Product owner: 3

Developers: 5

Testers: 8

Which action should the team agree on?

Answer:

A. As the developers are developing the system, the developer estimates should be taken as correct when there is a conflict.

B. The team should hold a conversation to understand why the testers and product owner gave different story points for the work required for the story. Another round of the planning poker session should occur following that discussion.

C. As the product owner owns the system, the customers' estimates should be taken as correct when there is a conflict.

D. The poker planning sessions should continue until all estimated story points are an exact match between product owner, developers, and testers.

Question 33

An agile team is assigned to a project to create a mobile interface for an existing web based application.

A few of the features are not supported in the mobile interface and the way a user can access the interface is also changing and will be documented in user stories.

Based on this information, and in addition to the user stories, which of the following would best provide relevant information to support your testing activities?

i.   Existing functions, features, and quality characteristics of the web based application

ii. Architecture diagrams for the web based application.

iii. Obsolete user access test cases for web based application.

iv. Performance metrics for existing application.

v.   Defects from existing and previous releases of the web based application.

Answer:

A. i, ii, iii, iv

B. i, ii, v

C. ii, iv, v

D. All of the above

Question 34

Which TWO of the following are examples of testable acceptance criteria for test related activities?

Answer:

A. 100% of decision coverage tested.

B. Good percentage of functional test is automated.

C. The user access is revoked after non activity of account.

D. The application is responding in less than 2 sec.

Question 35

Given the following User Story for an online banking feature:

"As a customer, I would like to update my daily limits for my transaction account so I can transfer up to $5000 to any other account on any given day, the limit options are $1000, $2000 & $5000"

Which of the following can be considered as relevant acceptance test cases?

i.   Login as a customer, check the customer can open transaction history page

ii.   Login as a customer, check the customer can transfer the money up to his daily limit

iii. Login as a customer, check the customer is not able to transfer money beyond his daily limit

iv   Login as a customer, check the daily limit dropdown have the options for $1000,$2000 & $5000

v.   Login as a customer the daily limit page should open in less than 2 seconds

Answer:

A.   i, ii, iv

B.   i, iii, iv

C.   ii, iv, v

D.   ii, iii, iv

Question 36

Given the following user story:

"A System to decide on the eligibility of getting the licence is based on the following criteria:

- If driver age is < 18 then eligibility is false

- If driver age is between 18 and 20 & driver training is true then eligibility = true

- If driver age is between 18 and 20 & driver training is false then eligibility = false

- If driver age is >20 then eligibility is true (training does not matter) "

Which of the following is the best black box test design technique for the user story?

Answer:

A. State Transition testing

B. Decision tables

C. Equivalence Partitioning

D. Use Case Testing.

Question 37

An Agile team is using Session-based test management for exploratory testing for one of the features which involves transferring files from a front- end system to a different system.

In the survey session, Testers have raised a few questions about what to test in the feature.

Which of the following testers' questions is NOT relevant to the exploratory testing?

Answer:

A. Which users can initiate the file transfer?

B. What is the performance requirement for the file transfer?

C. What are the various ways the users can trigger the file transfer from the front end?

D. What are the various ways the file transfer can fail?

Question 38

Which of the following is one of the purposes of a test Charter?

Answer:

A. Test Charter helps the testers in test data generation for testing

B. Test Charter guides the testers in exploratory testing

C. Test Charter provides a knowledge base on tools and techniques for development and testing activities

D. Test Charter provides a quick response about the build quality and details about code changes

Question 39

Agile team is looking for a tool to manage requirements and traceability; additional features should be managing dashboards on product status & recording conversations

Which of the following will be suitable for this purpose?

A.   Configuration Management (CM) tool

B.   Wiki

C.   Test Charter

D.   Continuous Integration (CI) tool

Question 40

Which of the following two statements are TRUE with respect to exploratory testing?

1.   Exploratory testing encompasses concurrent learning, test design, and execution.

2.   Exploratory testing is carried out by the developers.

3.   Exploratory test cases should be automated for maximum benefit.

4.   Exploratory testers should have a prior knowledge of the system under test.

Answer:

A.   1 and 4

B.   1 and 2

C.   2 and 4

D.   1 and 3

Correct Answers and cognitive levels

1	C	K1
2	A	K1
3	D	K2
4	A	K2
5	C	K2
6	D	K2
7	B	K1
8	D	K3
9	C	K2
10	D	K2
11	B	K2
12	B	K1
13	D	K1
14	B	K2
15	A	K2
16	C	K2
17	D	K2
18	B	K2
19	B	K2
20	A	K2

21	B	K2
22	C	K2
23	C	K2
24	D	K2
25	A	K1
26	C	K1
27	A	K1
28	D	K2
29	D	K2
30	B	K3
31	B	K3
32	B	K3
33	B	K3
34	A	K2
35	D	K3
36	B	K3
37	B	K3
38	B	K1
39	B	K1
40	A	K1

3. Agile Tester Extension Sample Exam 1 - Answer Sheet

Question 1

FA-1.1.1 (K1) Recall the basic concept of Agile software development based on the Agile Manifesto

Justification:

A. Incorrect – This is true – see (C) for correct answer

B. Incorrect – This is true – see (C) for correct answer

C. Correct – This is false. The Manifesto consists of 4 key values: Individuals and Interactions over processes and tools; Working software over comprehensive documentation; Customer collaboration over contract negotiation; Responding to change over following a plan

D. Incorrect – This is true – see (C) for correct answer

Question 2

FA-1.1.1 (K1) Recall the basic concept of Agile software development based on the Agile Manifesto

Justification:

A.   Correct – project teams that can respond quickly to customers, product users, and the market in general are able to develop relevant, helpful products that people want to use.

B.   Incorrect – It is normal practice in agile development, but it is not one of the values in the agile Manifesto.

C.   Incorrect – It is normal practice in agile development, but it is not one of the values in the agile Manifesto.

D.   Incorrect – It is normal practice in agile development, but it is not one of the values in the agile Manifesto.

Question 3

FA-1.1.2 (K2) Understand the advantages of the whole-team approach

Justification:

A.   Incorrect – Testers help the team in testing tasks but they are not responsible for quality as in traditional project development methods

B.   Incorrect – Developers develop the stories and help the team in automation

C.   Incorrect – The Business Analyst creates the acceptance criteria with the help of the team

D.   Correct - In agile projects, quality is the responsibility of the whole team

E.   Incorrect – The Product owner represents the business and provides frequent feedback to the team

Question 4

FA-1.1.2 (K2) Understand the advantages of the whole-team approach

Justification:

A.   correct – The whole-team approach is supported through the daily stand-up meetings involving all members of the team, where work progress is communicated and any impediments to progress are highlighted.

B.   Incorrect - Continuous integration has nothing to do with the whole team approach

C.   Incorrect – Test driven development has nothing to do with the whole team approach

D.   Incorrect – In pairing two team members (e.g., a tester and a developer, two testers, or a tester and a product owner sit together at one workstation to perform a testing or other sprint task) is not an example of the whole team approach

Question 5

FA-1.1.3 (K2) Understand the benefits of early and frequent feedback

Justification:

A.   Incorrect.

B.   Incorrect.

C.   Correct – See details below.

1.   Incorrect –Continuous integration is one way to provide rapid feedback not the only way.

2.   Correct – It is easy to check the work done in an iteration and see how it can be improved.

3.   Incorrect – bugs can be found early but not necessarily the high severity defects.

4.   Correct – Customers indicate if requirements are not met early, and modify functionality if required

D.   Incorrect.

Question 6

FA-1.1.3 (K2) Understand the benefits of early and frequent feedback

Justification:

A. Incorrect – This is true.

B. Incorrect – This is true.

C. Incorrect – This is true.

D. Correct –This is false as there may be more testing required due to frequent changes.

Question 7

FA-1.2.1 (K1) Recall Agile software development approaches

Justification:

A. Incorrect – see (B) for correct answer

B. correct – Quality is not the value in Extreme Programming development, five values to guide development are: communication, simplicity, feedback, courage, and respect.

C. Incorrect – see (B) for correct answer

D. Incorrect – see (B) for correct answer

E. Incorrect – see (B) for correct answer

Question 8

FA-1.2.2 (K3) Write testable user stories in collaboration with developers and business representatives

Justification:

A. Incorrect – It is not necessary that the increase in development effort will increase the testing effort.

B. Incorrect – The product owner will prioritize the story, the tester doesn't decide that.

C. Incorrect – Changes to performance testing requirements will be decided by the team, not the tester alone.

D. Correct – The tester should ensure that there is testable acceptance criteria for all of the functions of the user story.

Question 9

FA-1.2.3 (K2) Understand how retrospectives can be used as a mechanism for process improvement in Agile projects

Justification:

A. Incorrect – see (C) for correct answer

B. Incorrect – see (C) for correct answer

C. Correct – All team members, including testers, should provide input and feedback on both testing and non-testing activities in retrospective meetings

D. Incorrect – see (C) for correct answer

Question 10

FA-1.2.3 (K2) Understand how retrospectives can be used as a mechanism for process improvement in Agile projects

Justification:

A. Incorrect – see justification below.

B. Incorrect – see justification below.

C. Incorrect – see justification below.

D. Correct – see justification below.

    i.   Correct – This could be raised as a process improvement.

    ii.   Correct– This could be raised as a process improvement, this could improve the efficiency of team

    iii.   Correct– This could be raised as a process improvement.

    iv.   Correct – This could be raised, team activities can result in better communication and team efficiency.

Question 11

FA-1.2.4 (K2) Understand the use and purpose of continuous integration

A. Incorrect

B. Correct– See details below.

    1.   Correct –Continuous integration finds integration problems earlier, also conflicting changes when multiple people check in code at the same time are found during the process.

    2.   Correct – Continuous integration results provide the development team feedback on their code.

    3.   Incorrect – System testing is still required after the continuous integration.

    4.   Incorrect   Code check in is slow after continuous integration as additional automated tests are run during the process

C. Incorrect

D. Incorrect

Question 12

FA-1.2.5 (K1) Know the differences between iteration and release planning, and how a tester adds value to each activity

Justification:

A. Incorrect

B. Correct– See details below.

    1. False – This is expected during release planning.

    2. True – This is expected during iteration planning.

    3. True – This is expected during iteration planning.

    4. False – This is expected during release planning.

C. Incorrect

D. Incorrect

Question 13

Agile Extension-Term (K1)

Justification:

A. Incorrect – This is related to user story, Story Acceptance criteria is collaboration defined by business representatives, developers, and testers for each user story

B. Incorrect – This is related to user story, a Story point is assigned to each user story during the poker planning session.

C. Incorrect – This is related to user story, each user story is assigned a priority by the business users during release planning,

D. Correct – There is **no** Story Entry criteria.

Question 14

FA-2.1.1 (K2) Describe the differences between testing activities in Agile projects and non-Agile projects

Justification:

A. Incorrect –Lightweight documentation is favoured in Agile projects.

B. Correct – Test automation occurs at all levels in most agile teams. In Agile projects testers focus on automating, executing and maintaining tests on integration, system, and acceptance level. In traditional projects testers do not have the same focus on automation.

C. Incorrect – Defect based techniques such as software attacks and error guessing are used in traditional projects also.

D. Incorrect – risk based testing techniques are used in traditional projects also,

Question 15

FA-2.1.2 (K2) Describe how development and testing activities are integrated in Agile projects

Justification:

A. Correct – See details below.

B. Incorrect

C. Incorrect

D. Incorrect

i.   This is one of the Test work products.

ii. This is one of the Test work products.

iii. This is one of the business-oriented work products, not a Test work product.

iv. This is one of the developer work products, not a Test Work product.

Question 16

FA-2.1.3 (K2) Describe the role of independent testing in Agile projects

Justification:

A. Incorrect –The testers who are working on the iteration should be engaged in iteration related activities not the independent test team.

B. Incorrect –The testers who are working on the iteration should be engaged in release planning not the independent test team.

C. Correct – Independent testing team can carry out test levels e.g. system integration testing, that might not fit well within a sprint

D. Incorrect – Developers and testers work collaboratively to do the automation task during the sprints

Question 17

FA-2.1.3 (K2) Describe the role of independent testing in Agile projects

Justification:

A. Incorrect

B. Incorrect

C. Incorrect

D. Correct–- See details below.

1. True - Independent test teams can work on the iteration-independent activities like creating and supporting test environments and data

2. False - If the team will work on the iteration testing activities with the Agile team, then there is a chance to lose test independence.

3. True - Independent test teams can provide an objective, unbiased evaluation of the software at the end of a sprint.

4. False - If the team will work on the automation testing activities with the developers, then there is a chance to lose test independence.

Question 18

FA-2.2.1 (K2) Describe the tools and techniques used to communicate the status of testing in an Agile project, including test progress and product quality

Justification:

A. Incorrect – The Test status report shows the progress of testing and can be used to measure the progress of testing.

B. Correct – Burndown charts show the planned progress and release date together with the actual progress of the user stories.

C. Incorrect – Number of completed stories will tell the team velocity for that sprint.

D. Incorrect – The Test Summary report contains summary of test activities and final test results.

Question 19

FA-2.2.1 (K2) Describe the tools and techniques used to communicate the status of testing in an Agile project, including test progress and product quality

Justification:

A. Incorrect – The tester alone can't determine the stories for the next sprints. They should be addressed by the entire team during sprint planning.

B. Correct – Any issues that may block test progress should be communicated during the daily stand-up meetings so the whole team is made aware of the issue(s) and can work together to find suitable solution(s).

C. Incorrect – Automation activities are planned in parallel to testing activities, not during downtime.

D. Incorrect – Retrospectives cover topics such as the process, people, organizations, relationships, and tools. Blockers should be raised in daily stand-up meetings

Question 20

FA-2.2.2 (K2) Describe the process of evolving tests across multiple iterations and explain why test automation is important to manage regression risk in Agile projects Justification:

A. Correct – the automation acceptance test suit should be run at least daily.

B. Incorrect – see (A) for correct answer

C. Incorrect – the automation acceptance test suit should not be run with each code check-in as they take longer to run than automated unit tests and could slow down code check-in, see (A) for correct answer

D. Incorrect – see (A) for correct answer

Question 21

FA-2.2.2 (K2) Describe the process of evolving tests across multiple iterations, and explain why test automation is important to manage regression risk in Agile projects

Justification:

A. Incorrect- see (B) for detailed justification

B. Correct. Automation unit tests will provide rapid feedback on product quality and can reduce the risk of regression. Automation for test data generation, comparing data output and restoring test environment will allow the team to spend more time in developing and testing new features but will not reduce the risk of code churn.

C. Incorrect- see (B) for detailed justification

D. Incorrect- see (B) for detailed justification

Question 22

FA-2.3.1 (K2) Understand the skills (people, domain, and testing) of a tester in an Agile team

Justification:

A. Incorrect – see justification below.

B. Incorrect – see justification below.

C. Correct – see justification below.

D. Incorrect – see justification below

i. Correct   In agile, there is a lot of emphasis on automation tests so it is an essential skill for a tester.

ii. Incorrect– Alpha/beta Testing is done by customers. Testers can assist, but it is not a necessary skill.

iii. Correct – In agile, there is a lot of emphasis on exploratory testing so it is an essential skill for a tester.

iv. Incorrect– Unit Testing is done by developers. Testers can assist but it is not a necessary skill

Question 23

FA-2.3.2 (K2) Understand the role of a tester within an Agile team

Justification:

A. Incorrect – see justification below.

B. Incorrect – see justification below.

C. Correct – see justification below.

D. Incorrect – see justification below

i   Incorrect – This task is a collaborative effort for the whole team.

ii. Correct– This activity is expected of the agile tester.

iii. Incorrect – In agile, It is the Scrum Master's role to produce and update the burndown chart from the information supplied by the rest of the team

iv. Correct – This activity is typical for an agile tester.

v. Incorrect – The business users decide the priority on user stories.

Question 24

FA-2.3.2 (K2) Understand the role of a tester within an Agile team

Justification:

A. Incorrect – This is true, Agile organizations may encounter this test related risk.

B. Incorrect – This is true, Agile organizations may encounter this test related risk.

C. Incorrect – This is true, Agile organizations may encounter this test related risk.

D. Correct – This is not a test related organization risk.

Question 25

Agile Extension-Term (K1)

Justification:

A. Correct – This is true for velocity chart

B. Incorrect – This is a code coverage chart, not a velocity chart

C. Incorrect – This is a defect discover rate chart, not a velocity chart

D. Incorrect – This is a Code Churn chart, not a velocity chart.

Question 26

FA-3.1.1 (K1) Recall the concepts of test-driven development, acceptance test-driven development and behavior-driven development

Justification:

A. Incorrect – This is true of BDD.

B. Incorrect – This is true of BDD.

C. Correct – This is true of TDD – not BDD.

D. Incorrect – This is true of BDD.

Question 27

FA-3.1.2 (K1) Recall the concepts of the test pyramid

Justification:

A. Correct – The test levels from the base of the pyramid to the top are unit/ component, integration, system, and acceptance

B. Incorrect – see (A) for correct answer

C. Incorrect – see (A) for correct answer

D. Incorrect – see (A) for correct answer

Question 28

FA-3.1.3 (K2) Summarize the testing quadrants and their relationships with testing levels and testing types

Justification:

A. Incorrect – see below

B. Incorrect – see below

C. Incorrect – see below

D. Correct – see below

Quadrant Q1 is unit level, technology facing, and supports the developers.

Quadrant Q2 is system/functional level, business facing, and confirms product behavior

Quadrant Q3 is user acceptance level, business facing, and contains tests that critique the product

Quadrant Q4 is system or operational acceptance level, technology facing, and contains tests that critique the product.

Question 29

FA-3.1.3 (K2) Summarize the testing quadrants and their relationships with testing levels and testing types

Justification:

A. Incorrect – see below.

B. Incorrect – see below.

C. Incorrect – see below.

D. Correct – see below,

Q1 – Incorrect – These test cases are not technology-facing component tests.

Q2 – Correct – System level is part of the 2nd quadrant

Q3 – Incorrect – These test cases are not user acceptance level tests.

Q4 – Correct – Performance testing is part of the 4th quadrant.

Question 30

FA-3.1.4 (K3) For a given Agile project, practice the role of a tester in a Scrum team

Justification:

A. Incorrect – A risk analysis should be done including the whole team and a collaborative decision should be made.

B. Correct – The decision to modify the test automation framework and scripts should be done collaboratively with the whole team. The tester is then responsible to make changes to the iteration plan as required.

C. Incorrect – The tester must notify the team who will then decide what to do with the issue.

D. Incorrect – It is not up to the tester alone to determine the scope of work. This issue will be addressed by creating a new user story or modifying an existing user story, and will be addressed by the entire team during sprint planning.

Question 31

FA-3.2.1 (K3) Assess product quality risks within an Agile project Justification:

A. Incorrect- see justification below

B. Correct - see justification below

C. Incorrect - see justification below

D. Incorrect - see justification below

User Story 1: Calculation (accuracy) in report is a functional risk

User Story 2: Storing customer sensitive information is a security risk

User Story 3: Difficulty in understanding screens for the users (senior citizens) is a usability risk

Question 32

FA-3.2.2 (K3) Estimate testing effort based on iteration content and product quality risks

Justification:

A. Incorrect – The entire team must agree on the estimate for the user story. The developer alone does not understand the complexity of developing or testing the functionality.

B. Correct – Planning poker sessions should continue for the user story, until the entire team is satisfied with the estimated effort.

C. Incorrect – The entire team must agree on the estimate for the user story. The customer alone does not understand the complexity of developing or testing the functionality.

D. Incorrect – It is not necessary that they match, a rule could be made that the highest estimate is taken, or an average taken of all three estimates. This is up to the team to decide before the planning poker session

Question 33

FA-3.3.1 (K3) Interpret relevant information to support testing activities

Justification:

A. Incorrect – see below

B. Correct - see below

C. Incorrect - see below

D. Incorrect – see below

i. This is helpful to write the test cases

ii. This is helpful to understand the application and write test cases.

iii. This information is not helpful, since user access is changing with mobile interface and new user stories have been documented.

iv. Because of the new interface, baselines should be obtained using mobile devices or defined performance requirements for this type of technology.

v. This is helpful during the risk analysis phase.

Question 34

FA-3.3.2 (K2) Explain to business stakeholders how to define testable acceptance criteria

Justification:

A. Correct – This is testable.

B. Incorrect –This is not testable, this is an ambiguous statement because the percentage is not specified.

C. Incorrect – This is not testable, the period of non-activity is not specified.

D. Correct – This is testable.

Question 35

FA-3.3.3 (K3) Given a user story, write acceptance test-driven development test cases

Justification:

A. Incorrect – see justification below.

B. Incorrect – see justification below.

C. Incorrect – see justification below.

D. Correct – see justification below.

i. Incorrect – User story is specific to customers' daily limit change, not the transaction history.

ii. Correct – This test is specific to a customer and results in verifying the daily limit functionality is working fine.

iii. Correct – This test is specific to a customer and results in verifying the daily limit functionality is working fine.

iv. Correct -This test is specific to a customer and results in verifying the daily limit is set up correctly in system.

v. Incorrect – User story does not mention performance requirements.

Question 36

FA-3.3.4 (K3) For both functional and non-functional behavior, write test cases using black box test design techniques based on given user stories

Justification:

A. Incorrect – see (B) for correct answer

B. Correct – Decision tables are best for user stories where the Actions are based on the Conditions.

C. Incorrect   see (B) for correct answer

D. Incorrect – see (B) for correct answer.

Question 37

FA-3.3.5 (K3) Perform exploratory testing to support the testing of an Agile project

Justification:

A. Incorrect – This is a relevant question this will help in the design and execution of exploratory test

B. Correct – This question is not relevant for exploratory testing, this is helpful to design the performance tests.

C. Incorrect – This is a relevant question this will help in the design and execution of exploratory test

D. Incorrect – This is a relevant question this will help in the design and execution of exploratory test

Question 38

FA-3.4.1 (K1) Recall different tools available to testers according to their purpose and to activities in agile projects

Justification:

A. Incorrect – This would be one of the purposes of a data generation tool

B. Correct – This is one of many purposes of a Test Charter.

C. Incorrect – This would be one of the purposes of a Wiki.

D. Incorrect – This would be one of the purposes of a Continuous Integration (CI) tool

Question 39

FA-3.4.1 (K1) Recall different tools available to testers according to their purpose and to activities in agile projects

Justification:

A. Incorrect – A Configuration Management (CM) tool will be suitable for storing source code and other test work products

B. Correct – This is one of many purposes of a wiki tool.

C. Incorrect – A Test Charter will be suitable for exploratory testing.

D. Incorrect – A Continuous Integration (CI) tool will be suitable for visibility on build status and automatic reporting.

Question 40

Agile Extension-Term (K1)

Justification:

A. Correct – see justification below.

B. Incorrect – see justification below.

C. Incorrect – see justification below.

D. Incorrect – see justification below.

1. True - Exploratory testing encompasses concurrent learning, test design, and execution.

2. False - exploratory testing is carried out by testers

3. False - automation of exploratory testing is not possible as test design and execution happens in parallel

4. True - the tester needs a good understanding of how the system is used and how to determine when it fails

4. Agile Tester Extension Sample Exam 2

Question 1

Match the Agile Manifesto statements (1-4) below with its correct value (i-iv).

1. Responding to change

2. Customer collaboration

3. Individuals and interactions

4. Working software

i. Can help teams work most effectively.

ii. Improves the likelihood of understanding what the customer requires

iii. Provides the opportunity to give the development team rapid feedback.

iv. Can help teams develop a relevant product that the customer wants.

Answer:

A. 1 – iii, 2 – iv, 3 – ii, 4 – i

B. 1 – iii, 2 – ii, 3 – i, 4 – iv

C. 1 – iv, 2 – ii, 3 – i, 4 – iii

D. 1 – ii, 2 – iii, 3 – iv, 4 – i

Question 2

The statement 'Agile development is very "people-centered"' relates to which of the following Agile Manifesto values?

Answer:

A. Individuals and Interactions over processes and tools

B. Working software over comprehensive documentation;

C. Customer collaboration over contract negotiation;

D. Responding to change over following a plan.

Question 3

Which of the following is NOT a benefit of the whole team approach?

Answer:

A. Enhancing communication and collaboration within the team

B. Enabling the various skill sets within the team to be leveraged

C. Making quality everyone's responsibility

D. Specialized testers not required

Question 4

One of the new Agile teams has agreed to use the "power of three" concept to take advantage of the whole team approach. Which of the below statement relates to this?

Answer:

A. The concept involving scrum master, developers, and tester in all feature discussions

B. The concept of involving testers, developers, and business representatives in all feature discussions

C. The concept involving DBA, developers, and Architect in all feature discussions

D. The concept involving scrum master, business representatives, and tester in all feature discussions

Question 5

Which TWO of the following statements are true?

1. Early feedback helps the team focus on the features with the highest value or associated risk so they are delivered to the customer first.

2. Early feedback reduces the time needed for system testing because the quality problems are discovered and resolved early.

3. Early feedback helps in avoiding requirement misunderstanding because the customer sees the product regularly

4. Early feedback gives the testers more time to work on the features in the next iteration because they spend less time testing the features in the current iteration.

Answer:

A. 1 and 4

B. 2 and 3

C. 2 and 4

D. 1 and 3

Question 6

Which of the following is a benefit of early feedback in agile projects?

A. It helps to manage the team better.

B. It helps the team to deliver better quality software to the customer

C. Early feedback results in fewer changes to the software

D. Early feedback reduces the cost of the overall development cycle

Question 7

Which of the following is NOT related to the 'Scrum' software development approach?

Answer:

A. Sprint.

B. Definition of Done

C. Lead Time

D. Product Backlog

Question 8

During an iteration planning meeting, the team is discussing a user story for the new interface which will be integrated to external applications in later iterations. After the discussion the developers confirmed that they have enough information to start with their development work. The tester is not clear about some of the functionality which may be required for integration testing later. What should the tester do in this situation?

Answer:

A. As the Integration testing will be done later, the tester can confirm the functionality with the business representatives later.

B. The tester can collaborate with the developers to find out about the missing functionality once the coding is finished.

C. The tester should ask open ended questions to business representatives to confirm the acceptance criteria and the missing functionality as it may impact the testing.

D. The tester should not worry about the missing details as it is the team responsibility to provide all the details to the tester.

Question 9

Which of the following is NOT the purpose of retrospective meetings held at the end of each iteration?

Answer:

A. To discuss the team velocity and the ways to improve it.

B. To discuss the things during the iteration which were successful.

C. To discuss the things during the iteration which can be improved

D. To discuss how to incorporate the improvements and retain the success in future iterations.

Question 10

One of the Agile teams is using the "start, stop, continue" exercise for their iteration retrospective.

Which of the following is from the 'stop' list.

Answer:

A. Communicating better with each other

B. Accepting the story with incomplete requirements

C. Increase the coverage of Automation tests

D. Improve the performance of the test environment

Question 11

What is the correct sequence of activities for the continuous Integration process?

i. Compile

ii. Static code analysis

iii. Deploy

iv. Unit test

v. Integration test

vi. Report

A. i, ii, iii, iv, vi , v

B. ii, i, iv , iii, v, vi

C. ii, i, iv, , v , iii, v

D. v, ii, iii, iv, vi , i

Question 12

The tester collaborates with the team on which of the two following activities during release planning?

Answer:

A.   Specify the definition of "done"

B.   Creating testing tasks for user stories

C.   Testing of user stories.

D.   Test strategy for all test levels, addressing test scope and technical risks

Question 13

Which of the following is the characteristics of iterative development model which differentiates it from other development model?

Answer:

A.   Close collaboration between developers and testers

B.   Short iteration of development cycles

C.   Use of automation testing

D.   Testers involved in exploratory testing

Question 14

In one of the Agile projects there is heavy use of test automation, which TWO of the following techniques should testers use more for their manual testing?

i. Exploratory testing techniques.

ii. Static testing techniques

iii. Structure-based techniques

iv. Error guessing techniques.

Answer:

A. i and iv

B. i and iii

C. ii and iv

D. ii and iii

Question 15

Which TWO of the following statements are true on Agile projects?

Answer:

A. Feature verification testing, which is often automated, may be done by developers or testers

B. Regression testing can be done by the business users either at the close of each iteration, after the completion of each iteration, or after a series of iterations.

C. Feature validation testing is usually manual and can involve developers, testers, and business stakeholders working collaboratively

D. Acceptance testing can be done by developers, testers, and business stakeholders working collaboratively

Question 16

Which of the following statements about Independent testing on Agile projects is False?

Answer:

A.   Independent testing can be introduced at the start of a sprint.

B.   An Independent test team can be part of another team.

C.   There is a risk of losing test independence in Agile teams.

D.   An Independent test team can carry out test levels that might not fit within a sprint.

Question 17

Which TWO of the following testing tasks can be taken by the independent testing team on agile projects?

Answer:

A.   Non Functional testing

B.   Story level testing activities.

C.   System Integration testing.

D.   Story level automation activities.

Question 18

The Agile team wants to find out the overall product quality at the end of an iteration.

What is the best way of achieving this?

Answer:

A. The best way is to check with the testers as they should be able to assess quality based on their testing.

B. The best way is to check the burndown chart. If the team has successfully achieved the estimates, then the product quality is good.

C. The best way is to ask the customer to test the product to know whether the system works correctly and meets expectations.

D. The best way is to check the technical debt incurred so far. This will best indicate the product quality.

Question 19

Which of the following Two are the most popular tools and techniques to communicate the test progress to the team in an Agile project?

Answer:

A. Agile task board

B. Test Status report

C. Daily stand up meeting

D. Retrospectives

Question 20

The Agile team is developing the automated build verification tests to provide instant feedback on the software after deployment.

Which of the following TWO tests should be part of the Automated build verification tests?

1. All tests to cover critical system functionality.

2. All tests which has previously failed

3. All tests from the previous iteration

4. All tests to cover integration points.

Answer:

A. 2 and 3

B. 1 and 4

C. 2 and 4

D. 1 and 2

Question 21

Which TWO of the following statements justify high investment on Automation in Agile projects

i. Test Automation helps maintain velocity without incurring a large amount of technical debt.

ii. Test Automation helps to detect the defects early in the project cycle.

iii. Automated acceptance test results can provide immediate feedback on overall product quality.

iv. Test Automation gives the testers more time to test new features and functions in the current iteration.

v. Test Automation ensures that all test cases from the previous iterations are tested.

Answer:

A. i and v

B. i and iv

C. iii and iv

D. ii and v

Question 22

In Agile projects there is a greater need for testers to understand and be competent in white box testing.

Which TWO of the following reasons best indicate why this is a more important skill on Agile projects than on traditional projects?

i.   An Agile team is cross-functional so all members can help in each other's task. This also enables them to help developers.

ii. In Test Driven development testers have to write the unit test first so the developers can write the code.

iii. Agile testing relies more on white box testing than black box testing.

iv. Testers can improve the program logic by pair programming

v.   In Agile projects, testers often work closely with developers for automation of unit tests and review of code

Answer:

A.   i & ii

B.   ii & v

C.   iv & v

D.   i and v

Question 23

Which of the following is NOT a typical task performed by the tester on an Agile project?

Answer:

A.   To prepare and report the test coverage

B.   To prepare the test status report

C.   To produce the burndown charts

D.   To prepare the test strategy

Question 24

Which TWO of the following are activities for the Tester on Agile projects but not necessarily on traditional projects?

i.   Testers provide feedback on process quality.

ii.   Understand, implement and update the test strategy

iii.   Actively collaborate with developers and business stakeholders

iv.   Testers provide feedback on product quality.

v.   Automate and maintain Automation tests.

Answer:

A.   i & iii

B.   iii & v

C.   i & v

D.   ii and iv

Question 25

Which of the following is NOT used as an Agile metric?

Answer:

A.   Burndown chart

B.   Velocity Chart

C.   Code Churn chart

D.   Daily Status report

Question 26

Which of the following statements about Acceptance Test-Driven Development is FALSE?

Answer:

A. Acceptance Test-Driven Development allows a developer to focus on testing the code based on the expected behavior of the software.

B. Tests are created once the user story is analyzed, discussed and written by the Agile team.

C. Acceptance Test-Driven Development defines acceptance criteria and tests during the creation of the user stories.

D. Acceptance Test-Driven Development is a test-first approach, test cases are created prior to implementing the user story.

Question 27

What does the term 'Test Pyramid' refer to in Agile projects?

Answer:

A. It is used to help the team understand the testing coverage for the user story/ feature

B. It can help the team determine how much testing time will be required for each user story

C. The number of automated tests are greater at the unit level and decrease at the higher levels.

D. It can help the team to find the impacted automated tests due to changes in a feature

Question 28

Match the testing quadrants on the left (1-4) with its correct test type on the right (i-iv).

1.   1) Q1   i) Story test

2.   2) Q2   ii) Recovery test

3.   3) Q3   iii) Beta test

4.   4) Q4   iv) unit test

Answer:

A.   1 – iii, 2 – iv, 3 – ii, 4 – i

B.   1 – iv, 2 – ii, 3 – i, 4 – iii

C.   1 – iv, 2 – iii, 3 – i, 4 – ii

D.   1 – iv, 2 – i, 3 – iii, 4 – ii

Question 29

Given the following user story:

"The social networking application should now check for the user age and only the users of age 18 or above should be able to register "

And the associated test cases:

Test Case 1: Check the Save Method () saves the user age to the database.

Test Case 2: Verify an existing user is able to access the social networking site.

Test Case 3: A registered user is able to delete their social networking site account.

Which TWO test quadrants would the above test cases be part of?

Answer:

A.   Q1 unit level, technology facing & Q2 system level, business facing

B.   Q1 unit level, technology facing & Q3 system or user acceptance level, business facing

C.   Q3 system or user acceptance level, business facing & Q4 system or operation acceptance level, technology facing

D.   Q2 system level, business facing & Q4 system or operation acceptance level, technology facing

Question 30

In the New Agile team the testers and developers are sitting together but the product owners are based in a different location though they participate in all daily stand-up and planning meetings and retrospectives.

Some of the testers are new to the Agile project and they are not able to cope with the changes coming during each iteration. The product owner has found a couple of instances where the testing team has not followed the testing strategy agreed to by the team during test execution.

What organizational and behavioural best practices does the team lack?

Answer:

A.   Self-organizing, Empowered, credible

B.   Self-organizing, Resilience, committed

C.   Cross-functional, Empowered, credible

D.   Co-located, collaborative, committed

E.   Co-located, Resilience, Credible

Question 31

In the quality risk analysis session, ot iteration planning, the Agile team identified the quality risk for each story and the level of risk based on the impact and likelihood of defects

- User story 1(Functional): likelihood: high, impact: high

- User story 2(Security): likelihood: low, impact: medium

- User story 3(Performance): likelihood: high, impact: medium

- User story 4(Functional): likelihood: low, impact: low

- User story 5(Recoverability): likelihood: low, impact: medium

How can the team mitigate these risks during the iteration? Select TWO options.

Answer:

A.   The tasks associated with user story 1 should be started first.

B.   The tasks associated with user story 4 should be started last.

C.   The tasks associated with user story 3 should be started first.

D.   The tasks associated with user story 2 should be started last.

E.   The tasks associated with user story 5 should be started last.

Question 32

In a Planning Poker session the team is estimating the effort for User story 1 and User story 2 which are related to the same feature.

The team has agreed on the story points for user story 1 but during the discussion of user story 2 the tester realized that he is not aware of the additional information about the business rules and external interfaces which may increases the testing effort for user story 1.

What should the tester do in this situation?

Answer:

A. As the estimation is already done for user story 1, its better to raise the estimate for user story 2 this will compensate for the additional effect for the User story 1.

B. The tester should ask the team for a re-estimation of user story 1 based on the additional information.

C. The tester should raise his concern with the scrum master after the planning session and ask for an increase in the estimation.

D. The tester should not worry about the additional information as this was only an estimate anyway.

Question 33

An agile team is working on a project for a new payment application. Which of the following would best provide relevant information to support testing activities In addition to the user stories for the testing of new payment messages from the payer to the payee?

i.   Updated standard documents for existing payment applications.

ii. Information about the data schema and how the data is stored in database

iii. Architecture diagrams for the new payment application.

iv. Performance metrics for a similar payment application.

v.   Defects from an existing payment applications.

Answer:

A.   i, ii, iii, v

B.   i, ii, iv

C.   ii, iv, v

D.   All of the above

Question 34

Which of the following is NOT an example of a valid acceptance criteria for the user story?

Answer:

A.   Acceptance criteria to confirm the correct behaviour without exception or error conditions.

B.   Acceptance criteria to cover the behaviour with exceptions and error conditions

C.   Acceptance criteria to cover the usability attribute of the user story.

D.   Acceptance criteria to cover the characteristics not documented in the user story.

Question 35

The following is a User Story for an online, money transfer application's Receiver Bank Account:

"**As** an online banking customer **When** I am initiating an online money transfer, **Then** the system should validate the Bank code and Bank Account Number of the Receiver and notify if they are invalid"

Which of the following are relevant acceptance test cases?

i. Login as a customer, enter an invalid bank code to see the error message

ii. Login as a customer, check the customer account balance is displaying correctly before and after the transfer.

iii. Login as a customer, enter a valid bank code and bank account number , no error message should be displayed.

iv. Login as a customer, enter an invalid bank account number to see the error message.

v. Login as a customer, enter an valid bank code to see the Bank name from the list.

Answer:

A. i, ii, iv

B. i, iii, iv

C. ii, iv, v

D. ii, iii, iv

Question 36

Given the following user story:

An application calculates the variable interest rate for a bank account based on the following criteria:

- 1.5 percent for the first $1,000 credit
- 2.0 percent for the next $1,000
- 1.5 percent for the rest.

Which of the following is the best black box test design technique for the user story?

Answer:

A. State Transition testing: Test the following states for Account – First credit, Second credit, Rest.

B. Decision tables: Test the following conditions – User credit first $1000; Interest calculated as 1.5 % etc.

C. Boundary Value Analysis: Test the following boundaries – 1000,1001,2000,2001

D. Use Case Testing: Actor=customer; Prerequisites=customer has account, deposit amount ; Post conditions= Interest calculated

Question 37

In one of the Agile projects, testers have been asked to plan exploratory testing.

Which of the following approaches is NOT correct for Exploratory testing?

A. Testers will do the risk analysis and test the critical things the tester and user think could go wrong or the potential problems that will make people unhappy.

B. Testers will test based on the model of how software should behave. The functions which the customers are more interested in should be tested first.

C. Testers will test based on their past experience of how similar systems failed in predictable patterns. These experiences can be refined into a test and explored.

D. Tests will not be planned as the testers have already tested these stories and should progress the test based on their intuition.

Question 38

Which of the following is NOT a purpose of a continuous Integration (CI) tool on an Agile project?

Answer:

A. To provide quick feedback of code quality

B. To provide assistance to testers for integration testing

C. To provide quick response about the build quality and details about code changes

D. To provide automatic reporting

Question 39

An Agile team wants to provide traceability between versions of software and the tests used. Which tool will be beneficial for the team?

Answer:

A. Continuous Integration (CI) tool

B. Wiki

C. ALM

D. Configuration management(CM) tool

Question 40

Which statement is TRUE in respect to exploratory testing in Agile projects?

Answer:

A. Testers having good knowledge of the system should perform exploratory testing.

B. The Independent Test team should be engaged in exploratory testing

C. Users engaged in Alpha testing should perform exploratory testing

D. Automated tests should be used for exploratory testing.

Correct Answers and cognitive levels

1	C	K1		21	B	K2
2	A	K1		22	D	K2
3	D	K2		23	C	K2
4	B	K2		24	C	K2
5	D	K2		25	D	K1
6	A	K2		26	A	K1
7	C	K1		27	C	K1
8	C	K3		28	D	K2
9	A	K2		29	B	K2
10	B	K2		30	E	K3
11	B	K2		31	A, B	K3
12	A	K1		32	B	K3
13	B	K1		33	D	K3
14	A	K2		34	D	K2
15	A	K2		35	B	K3
16	A	K2		36	C	K3
17	A	K2		37	D	K3
18	C	K2		38	B	K1
19	A,C	K2		39	D	K1
20	B	K2		40	A	K1

5. Agile Tester Extension Sample Exam 2 - Answer Sheet

Question 1

FA-1.1.1 (K1) Recall the basic concept of Agile software development based on the Agile Manifesto

Justification:

A. Incorrect –see (C) for correct answer

B. Incorrect –see (C) for correct answer

C. Correct –

Project teams that can respond quickly develop relevant products that the customers want;

Close collaboration with the customer help in understanding the customer's requirements better;

As Agile development is people-centered through continuous communication and interaction teams can work most effectively;

From the customer's perspective, working software is useful and valuable and it provides an opportunity to give the development team rapid feedback;

D. Incorrect – see (C) for correct answer

Question 2

FA-1.1.1 (K1) Recall the basic concept of Agile software development based on the Agile Manifesto

Justification:

A. Correct – Agile development put strong emphasis on Individual communication and interaction in comparison to reliance on tools or processes so the teams can work most effectively.

B. Incorrect – see (A) for correct answer

C. Incorrect – see (A) for correct answer

D. Incorrect – see (A) for correct answer

Question 3

FA-1.1.2 (K2) Understand the advantages of the whole-team approach

Justification:

A. Incorrect – True

B. Incorrect – True

C. Incorrect – True.

D. Correct – False, specialized testers are still needed on agile projects.

Question 4

FA-1.1.2 (K2) Understand the advantages of the whole-team approach

Justification:

A. Incorrect – see (B) for correct answer

B. correct – The concept of involving testers, developers, and business representatives in any discussions or meetings in which product features are presented, analyzed, or estimated is known as the power of three.

C. Incorrect – see (B) for correct answer

D. Incorrect – see (B) for correct answer

Question 5

FA-1.1.3 (K2) Understand the benefits of early and frequent feedback

Justification:

A. Incorrect.

B. Incorrect.

C. Incorrect.

D. Correct – See details below

1. Correct – Frequent customer feedback maintains a focus on the features with the highest business value or associated risk

2. Incorrect – There may be more system testing required due to frequent changes.

3. Correct – Since the customer is checking the product early and regularly there is less chance of requirement misunderstanding.

4. Incorrect – Testers will work on the features included in the current iteration. If they complete their testing, they will help out the other team members.

Question 6

FA-1.1.3 (K2) Understand the benefits of early and frequent feedback

Justification:

A. Correct –As the capability of the team is transparent to everyone It is easy to manage the team better.

B. Incorrect – Early feedback avoids requirement misunderstanding but not necessarily results in better quality of software.

C. Incorrect –There may be more changes due to early feedback.

D. Incorrect –There may be more testing required due to frequent changes.

Question 7

FA-1.2.1 (K1) Recall Agile software development approaches

Justification:

A. Incorrect – True. Scrum divides a project into iterations (called sprints) of fixed length.

B. Incorrect – True. Definition of Done is the appropriate criteria for sprint completion decided by the scrum team.

C. Correct – False. This is used in kanban to optimize the continuous flow of tasks

D. Incorrect – True. The product owner manages a prioritized list of planned product items (called the product backlog).

Question 8

FA-1.2.2 (K3) Write testable user stories in collaboration with developers and business representatives

Justification:

A. Incorrect – The tester should confirm the functionality during the planning meeting, not later.

B. Incorrect – The tester should ask questions to confirm the functionality during the planning meeting.

C. Correct – It is the responsibility of the tester to ask all questions about the missing functionality as this may result in complexities the team has not thought about.

D. Incorrect – The tester should make sure that all information is there for testing the story.

Question 9

FA-1.2.3 (K2) Understand how retrospectives can be used as a mechanism for process improvement in Agile projects

Justification:

A. Correct –False- The purpose of retrospective meeting is not to discuss team velocity or ways to improve it.

B. Incorrect – True - one of the purposes of a retrospective meeting is to find out the things which were successful.

C. Incorrect – True - one of the purposes of a retrospective meeting is to find out the things which can be improved.

D. Incorrect – True - one of the purposes of a retrospective meeting is to incorporate the improvements in future iterations.

Question 10

FA-1.2.3 (K2) Understand how retrospectives can be used as a mechanism for process improvement in Agile projects

Justification:

A. Incorrect – This is from the 'continue' list

B. Correct – This is from the 'stop' list. The team should stop accepting the stories without complete requirements.

C. Incorrect – This is from the 'start' list

D. Incorrect – This is from the 'start' list

Question 11

FA-1.2.4 (K2) Understand the use and purpose of continuous integration

A. Incorrect – see (B) for correct answer

B. Correct – The Continuous integration process consists of the following automated activities:

• Static code analysis: executing static code analysis and reporting the results

• Compile: compiling and linking the code, generating the executable files

• Unit test: executing the unit tests, checking code coverage and reporting the test results

• Deploy: installing the build into a test environment

• Integration test: executing the integration tests and reporting the results

• Report (dashboard): posting the status of all these activities to a publicly visible location or emailing the status to the team.

C. Incorrect – see (B) for correct answer

D. Incorrect – see (B) for correct answer

Question 12

FA-1.2.5 (K1) Know the differences between iteration and release planning, and how a tester adds value to each activity

A. Correct – This is an activity during release planning

B. Incorrect – This is an activity during iteration planning

C. Incorrect – This is an activity during iteration planning

D. Correct – This is an activity during release planning

Question 13

Agile Extension-Term (K1)

Justification:

A. Incorrect – This can happen in other traditional development methods also.

B. Correct – An Agile project consists of short iterations of development vs. a long development cycle in a traditional method.

C. Incorrect –Automation testing is also likely to take place in other traditional development methods based on the project's needs.

D. Incorrect – Exploratory testing is also likely to take place in other traditional development methods.

Question 14

FA-2.1.1 (K2) Describe the differences between testing activities in Agile projects and non-Agile projects

Justification:

A. Correct – see justification below.

B. Incorrect – see justification below.

C. Incorrect – see justification below.

D. Incorrect – see justification below.

i. Exploratory testing techniques will be ideal for manual testing.

ii. Static testing techniques are used for testing code or requirements before the manual testing starts.

iii. Structure testing should be covered in Automated tests.

iv. Error testing techniques will be ideal for manual testing.

Question 15

FA-2.1.2 (K2) Describe how development and testing activities are integrated in Agile projects

Justification:

A. Correct – Feature verification testing involves testing against the user story's acceptance criteria and is done by developers or testers.

B. Incorrect – Regression testing should be done by tester not the business user.

C. Correct – Feature validation testing involves developers, testers, and business stakeholders working collaboratively to determine whether the feature is fit for use.

D. Incorrect – Acceptance testing is done by the customer

Question 16

FA-2.1.3 (K2) Describe the role of independent testing in Agile projects

Justification:

A. Correct – False. During the start of iterations there is more of a need for testers to work closely with developers; so there is a chance to lose test independence.

B. Incorrect – True. This option is satisfied when there are some specialized testers working on iteration independent or long term activities like developing an automated test tool or non functional testing etc.

C. Incorrect – True. This can happen when testers work closely with developers.

D. Incorrect – True. An Independent testing team can carry out test levels e.g. system integration testing, that might not fit well within a sprint

Question 17

FA-2.1.3 (K2) Describe the role of independent testing in Agile projects

Justification:

A. Correct – An Independent testing team can work on non functional testing which is an iteration-independent activity.

B. Incorrect – Story level testing involves working closely with the developer so there is a chance to lose test independence.

C. Correct – An Independent testing team can work on the test levels like system integration testing that might not fit well within a sprint.

D. Incorrect – Automation testing activities involve working closely with the developer so there is a chance to lose test independence.

Question 18

FA-2.2.1 (K2) Describe the tools and techniques used to communicate the status of testing in an Agile project, including test progress and product quality

Justification:

A. Incorrect – Test results may not necessarily indicate the product quality. It is important to know if the product meets the customer's expectations.

B. Incorrect – Burndown charts only show the planned progress and release date together with the actual progress of the user stories which is not an indicator of quality.

C. Correct –Customer feedback and working software are key indicators to product quality.

D. Incorrect – Technical debt may not necessarily indicate product quality. It is important to know if the product meets the customer's expectations.

Question 19

FA-2.2.1 (K2) Describe the tools and techniques used to communicate the status of testing in an Agile project, including test progress and product quality

Justification:

A. Correct – To provide the detailed visual representation of the whole team's current status, including status of testing, teams use Agile task boards.

B. Incorrect –Test status reports are not used for communicating test progress within the Agile team. They may be used for other metrics.

C. Correct – Daily stand up meetings provide the opportunity for testers to communicate test progress, including issues that may block test progress.

D. Incorrect – Retrospectives are not for status reporting. They are used to discuss topics such as the process, people, organizations, relationships, and tools.

Question 20

FA-2.2.2 (K2) Describe the process of evolving tests across multiple iterations and explain why test automation is important to manage regression risk in Agile projects

Justification:

A. Incorrect.

B. Correct– See details below

C. Incorrect.

D. Incorrect

1. Correct – All tests to cover critical system functionality should be part of the Automated build verification tests to make sure that the build is stable for testing.

2. Incorrect – All tests which have previously failed are not necessarily part of the Automated build verification tests.

3. Incorrect – All tests from the previous iteration are not necessarily part of the Automated build verification tests.

4. Correct – All tests to cover integration should be part of the Automated build verification tests to make sure that the build is stable for testing.

Question 21

FA-2.2.2 (K2) Describe the process of evolving tests across multiple iterations, and explain why test automation is important to manage regression risk in Agile projects

Justification:

A. Incorrect.

B. Correct - see below for detailed justification

C. Incorrect.

D. Incorrect.

i.   True - Changes in each iteration will require more and more regression testing. If automation was not used, then the team's velocity would be reduced or the Technical debt will increase.

ii. False - This is not a reason to introduce automation on a project.

iii. False - Automated acceptance test results can provide feedback on product quality with respect to the regression since the last build but they do not provide status of overall product quality.

iv. True - Automation reduces the regression test effort so the testers can work on other tasks from the current iteration.

v.   False - It is not feasible to automate all the tests and it is not possible to retest/ rerun all the test cases from all the previous iterations.

Question 22

FA-2.3.1 (K2) Understand the skills (people, domain, and testing) of a tester in an Agile team

Justification:

A. Incorrect – see justification below.

B. Incorrect – see justification below.

C. Incorrect – see justification below.

D. Correct – see justification below

i. Correct – True

ii. Incorrect – In TDD, Automated unit tests are written by the developers, not by testers.

iii. Incorrect – Agile projects require both white box and black box testing.

iv. Incorrect – Pair programming is typically done using two developers; testers are not expected to improve program logic.

v. Correct - True

Question 23

FA-2.3.2 (K2) Understand the role of a tester within an Agile team

Justification:

A. Incorrect – True - This activity is expected of the agile tester.

B. Incorrect – True - This activity is expected of the agile tester.

C. Correct – False - In agile, it is the Scrum Master's responsibility to produce and update the burndown chart based on the information given by the rest of the team

D. Incorrect – True - This activity is expected of the agile tester.

Question 24

FA-2.3.2 (K2) Understand the role of a tester within an Agile team

Justification:

A. Incorrect – see justification below.

B. Incorrect – see justification below.

C. Correct – see justification below.

D. Incorrect – see justification below

i. Correct – In agile, Testers provide feedback on process quality by proactively participating in the team retrospectives, suggesting and implementing improvements.

ii. Incorrect– This is required for both Agile and traditional projects.

iii. Incorrect– This is required for both Agile and traditional projects.

iv. Incorrect– This is required for both Agile and traditional projects.

v. Correct– In agile, automation is required, therefore part of the tester's role is to produce automation scripts, run and maintain them.

Question 25

Agile Extension-Term (K1)

Justification:

A. Incorrect – True – A Burndown chart is one of the Agile metrics. It shows the amount of work left to be done, versus the time allocated for the iteration.

B. Incorrect – True – Velocity chart is one of the Agile metrics. It shows the sum of the estimates of the work delivered across iterations. This may be used while selecting the stories for the next iteration.

C. Incorrect – True – Code Churn is one of the Agile metrics. It shows the number of defects discovered during a given period. This may be used as criteria for stopping the testing.

D. Correct – False -Daily status is not one of the Agile metrics. The team shares the status in the daily stand-up meetings.

Question 26

FA-3.1.1 (K1) Recall the concepts of test-driven development, acceptance test-driven development and behavior-driven development

Justification:

A. Correct – This is true of Behaviour Driven Development(BDD), not Acceptance Test-Driven Development.

B. Incorrect – This is true of Acceptance Test-Driven Development.

C. Incorrect – This is true of Acceptance Test-Driven Development.

D. Incorrect – This is true of Acceptance Test-Driven Development.

Question 27

FA-3.1.2 (K1) Recall the concepts of the test pyramid

Justification:

A. Incorrect – The workload for each sprint has nothing to do with the Test Pyramid concept.

B. Incorrect – The testing time for each user story has nothing to do with the Test Pyramid concept.

C. Correct – The test pyramid emphasizes having more tests at the lower levels and a decreasing number of tests at the higher levels.

D. Incorrect – The number of impacted automated tests due to changes in a feature has nothing to do with the Test Pyramid concept.

Question 28

FA-3.1.3 (K2) Summarize the testing quadrants and their relationships with testing levels and testing types

Justification:

A.   Incorrect – see below

B.   Incorrect – see below

C.   Incorrect – see below

D.   Correct – see below

Quadrant Q1 contains unit tests.

Quadrant Q2 contains functional tests, examples, story tests, user experience prototypes, and simulations.

Quadrant Q3 contains exploratory testing, scenarios, process flows, usability testing, user acceptance testing, alpha testing, and beta testing.

Quadrant Q4 contains performance, load, stress, and scalability tests, security tests, maintainability, memory management, compatibility and interoperability, data migration, infrastructure, and recovery testing

Question 29

FA-3.1.3 (K2) Summarize the testing quadrants and their relationships with testing levels and testing types

Justification:

A. Incorrect – see below.

B. Correct – see below.

C. Incorrect – see below.

D. Incorrect – see below,

Q1 – Correct – unit/component tests are part of 1st quadrant.

Q2 – Incorrect – These test cases are not system level tests.

Q3 – Correct – These test cases are for user acceptance level tests.

Q4 – Incorrect – These test cases are not for operation acceptance level tests

Question 30

FA-3.1.4 (K3) For a given Agile project, practice the role of a tester in a Scrum team

Justification:

A. Incorrect – see (E) for correct answer

B. Incorrect – see (E) for correct answer

C. Incorrect – see (E) for correct answer

D. Incorrect – see (E) for correct answer

E. Correct –

Co-located: Testers sit together with the developers and the product owner.

Resilience: Testing must be able to respond to changes.

Credible: The tester must ensure the credibility of the testing strategy.

Question 31

FA-3.2.1 (K3) Assess product quality risks within an Agile project Justification:

A. Correct - User story 1 has the highest level of risk so it should be started first.

B. Correct – User story 4 has the lowest level of risk so it should be started last.

C. Incorrect -User story 3 does not have the highest level of risk.

D. Incorrect -User story 2 does not have the lowest level of risk.

E. Incorrect -User story 5 does not have the lowest level of risk.

Question 32

FA-3.2.2 (K3) Estimate testing effort based on iteration content and product quality risks

Justification:

A. Incorrect – The estimate is given for each story and should be agreed upon by the entire team.

B. Correct – The tester should ask the team to re-estimate. Additional information about business rules may affect the development and testing effort.

C. Incorrect – The entire team must agree on the estimate for the user story. The scrum master and the tester can't decide on their own.

D. Incorrect – If there is additional information, then the whole team should be aware of it and it should be used to re-estimate the story.

Question 33

FA-3.3.1 (K3) Interpret relevant information to support testing activities

Justification:

A.   Incorrect – see below

B.   Incorrect – see below

C.   Incorrect – see below.

D.   Correct – see below

i.   This is helpful to write the test cases

ii.   This is helpful to understand the application and write E2E test cases.

iii.   This is helpful to understand the application and write test cases.

iv.   This is helpful during the risk analysis phase.

v.   This is helpful during the risk analysis phase.

Question 34

FA-3.3.2 (K2) Explain to business stakeholders how to define testable acceptance criteria

Justification:

A.   Incorrect – This is a valid example of the positive test.

B.   Incorrect – This is a valid example of the negative test.

C.   Incorrect – This is a valid example of the non functional test.

D.   Correct – This is not a valid example. The acceptance criteria should not describe an aspect of the user story not documented in the story itself.

Question 35

FA-3.3.3 (K3) Given a user story, write acceptance test-driven development test cases

Justification:

A. Incorrect – see justification below.

B. Correct – see justification below.

C. Incorrect – see justification below.

D. Incorrect – see justification below.

i. Correct – This test is specific to check the bank code and bank account number validation.

ii. Incorrect – The User story does not mention Account balance checks.

iii. Correct – This test is specific to check the bank code and bank account number validation.

iv. Correct- This test is specific to check the bank code and bank account number validation.

v. Incorrect – The User story does not mention displaying the Bank Name when entering a valid Bank code.

Question 36

FA-3.3.4 (K3) For both functional and non-functional behavior, write test cases using black box test design techniques based on given user stories

Justification:

A. Incorrect – The focus of this user story is not on the state of the system; instead the expectation is to test the right interest is calculated based on the account balance.

B. Incorrect – The focus of this user story is not on interest calculated, the expectation is to test the right interest is calculated based on the account balance.

C. Correct – BVA is the best option when testing different boundaries.

D. Incorrect – The focus of this user story is not on whether the Interest is calculated; the expectation is to test the right interest is calculated based on the account balance.

Question 37

FA-3.3.5 (K3) Perform exploratory testing to support the testing of an Agile project

Justification:

A. Incorrect – This is true for exploratory testing.

B. Incorrect – This is true for exploratory testing.

C. Incorrect – This is true for exploratory testing.

D. Correct – False - There is a plan required for exploratory testing.

Question 38

FA-3.4.1 (K1) Recall different tools available to testers according to their purpose and to activities in agile projects

Justification:

A. Incorrect – True - This would be one of the purposes of continuous Integration tools (CI) tool.

B. Correct – False - This is not the purposes of a Continuous Integration (CI) tool

C. Incorrect – True - This would be one of the purposes of a Continuous Integration (CI) tool.

D. Incorrect – True - This would be one of the purposes of a Continuous Integration (CI) tool.

Question 39

FA-3.4.1 (K1) Recall different tools available to testers according to their purpose and to activities in agile projects

Justification:

A.   Incorrect – Continuous Integration (CI) tools provide quick response about the build quality and details about code changes.

B.   Incorrect- Wiki allows teams to build a knowledge base on tools and techniques for development and testing activities

C.   Incorrect – An ALM tool provides visibility into the current state of the application, especially with distributed teams. It can provide traceability for the test used but not for version of software.

D.   Correct –Configuration management (CM) tools are suitable for providing traceability between versions of software and the tests used

Question 40

Agile Extension-Term (K1)

Justification:

A.   Correct – True - the tester needs good understanding of how the system is used

B.   Incorrect – False - exploratory testing is carried out by testers having good knowledge of the system so they can get the desired results in limited time.

C.   Incorrect – False - Exploratory testing is done before the user acceptance phase.

D.   Incorrect – False - automation of exploratory testing is not possible as test design and execution happens in parallel

6. Agile Tester Extension Sample Exam 3

Question 1

Which of the following is NOT an Agile Manifesto statement of values?

Answer:

1. Contract negotiation over customer collaboration
2. Responding to change over following a plan
3. Individuals and interactions over Processes and tools
4. Working software over Comprehensive documentation

Question 2

One of the Core Agile principles "Business people and developers must work together daily throughout the project" relates to which of the following Agile Manifesto values?

Answer:

A. Individuals and Interactions
B. Working software
C. Customer collaboration
D. Responding to change

Question 3

Which **TWO** of the following activities represent tasks and responsibilities that are consistent with the whole team approach in Agile projects?

Answer:

A. Testers create user stories for the team.

B. Testers are responsible to test functional requirements and developers are responsible to test non functional requirements

C. Testers collaborate with other team members for tasks related to building infrastructure and designing for testability.

D. Every team member on an Agile team takes responsibility for testing tasks.

E. Testers prioritize and estimate the user stories.

Question 4

Which of the following activities are **not** consistent with Agile's whole team approach?

Answer:

A. Testers working with the team in user story creation.

B. Product owner working on testing tasks.

C. Testers working on non-testing tasks.

D. Product owner and developers having discussion regarding user story.

Question 5

Which TWO of the following statements are true?

1. Early feedback results in inconsistent project momentum.

2. Early feedback ensures that the product better reflects what the customer wants

3. Early feedback reduces the time needed for testing because there are no requirement misunderstandings.

4. Early feedback helps to find quality problems early.

Answer:

A. 1 and 4

B. 2 and 3

C. 2 and 4

D. 1 and 3

Question 6

Which of the following can be used to take advantage of early and frequent feedback in Agile projects?

A. Involving business representatives in team planning meeting.

B. Involving testers in non testing tasks based on their skillsets.

C. Asking Developer to work on automation tasks

D. Asking customer to see the product regularly.

Question 7

Match the following terms on the top with their corresponding best agile software development on the bottom.

1. Pair programming, test first programming

2. backlog, sprints

3. work-in progress limit, lead time

i.   Kanban

ii. Extreme Programming(XP)

iii. Scrum

Answer:

A. 1-i, 2-iii, 3-ii

B. 1-i, 2-ii, 3-iii

C. 1-ii, 2-iii, 3-i

D. 1-iii, 2-ii, 3-i

Question 8

Which of the following roles are NOT defined according to the Scrum software development approach?

Answer:

A. Scrum Master

B. Product Owner

C. Development Team

D. Testing Team

Question 9

During an iteration planning meeting, the team is sharing their thoughts about an user story. The tester has asked the following to the product owner to add more clarity to the business value of the feature. Which of the following questions don't add any value to the discussion?

Answer:

A. The tester advises that the non-functional characteristics should be defined for the user story.

B. The tester advises that the user story needs acceptance criteria to be testable.

C. The tester asking open ended question regarding the missing details.

D. The tester advises that usability is more important than performance.

Question 10

Which of the following items should NOT be raised during a retrospective meeting?

Answer:

A. Test data creation taking a long time. There should be an automated process to create test data.

B. Developers not finishing the development activities on time.

C. The percentage of automation tests need to be increased to reduce regression risks.

D. The Test environment is slow and frequently unavailable for testing.

Question 11

Which TWO of the following are risks to the Continuous Integration process?

1. Continuous Integration increases the manual testing activities.

2. It increases the regression risk associated with developer code refactoring.

3. Continuous integration tools have to be introduced and maintained

4. Test automation requires additional resources and can be complex to establish

Answer:

A. 1 and 4

B. 1 and 2

C. 2 and 3

D. 3 and 4

Question 12

Which one of the following activities will a tester be involved with during iteration planning?

Answer:

A. Discuss the Test approach and test plan with the Team.

B. Determining the testability of the user stories.

C. Estimate testing tasks generated by new features planned for this iteration.

D. Support the clarification of the user stories and ensure that they are testable.

Question 13

Who is responsible for writing the 'user story' in Agile projects?

Answer:

A.   It is the tester's responsibility to write the user stories.

B.   It is the scrum master's responsibility to write the user stories for the team.

C.   It is the product owner's responsibility to write the user stories for the team.

D.   User stories are written collaboratively by developers, testers, and business representatives.

Question 14

What of the following is the purpose of hardening or stabilization iterations in Agile projects?

Answer:

A.   It is used to resolve any lingering defects and other forms of technical debts.

B.   It is used for customer testing so the team can get the feedback on product quality.

C.   It is used to finish any pending automation tasks to achieve desired test coverage.

D.   It is used for the team to work on process improvement activities.

Question 15

Which of the following combination of activities should occur in an Agile project?

i.   Functional verification testing of user stories developed in the previous iteration.

ii. Tester, developer, and business representative working collaboratively to determine whether the feature is fit for use.

iii. Re-running the automated unit tests and feature verification tests from the current iteration and previous iteration.

iv. System test level entry and exit criteria.

Answer:

A. ii and iv

B. i and ii

C. ii and iii

D. ii only

Question 16

Which of the following is an example of an independent test team in an Agile project?

Answer:

A. On-demand Testers working during the final days of each sprint.

B. Testers implementing and updating test strategy.

C. Testers working on iteration automation activities.

D. Testers working with team to write the user story.

Question 17

Which of the following testing tasks should NOT be taken by the independent testing team on Agile projects?

Answer:

A.   System Integration testing.

B.   Test data creation.

C.   Non Functional testing

D.   User story acceptance testing.

Question 18

Match the following tools used in Agile projects with their corresponding use on the bottom:

1.   Wiki dashboards

2.   Daily Stand-up meeting

3.   Customer satisfaction survey

4.   Agile Task boards

i.   To know product quality

ii.   To get team current status

iii.   To generate status report

iv.   To know team issues

Answer:

A.   1-iv, 2-ii, 3-i, 4-ii

B.   1-iv, 2-i, 3-ii, 4-iii

C.   1-ii, 2-iv, 3-ii, 4-i

A.   1-iii, 2-iv, 3-i, 4-ii

Question 19

The team has selected 3 stories in the current sprint each of them are 8 points, sprint size is 2 week. Sprint burndown chart will start with which of the following values in Y axis of burndown chart ?

Answer:

A. 24

B. 2

C. 8

D. 3

Question 20

Which of the following would need to be done first to minimize the introduction of regression risk when a feature which has already been delivered is changed in the current iteration?

Answer:

A. The team should increase the amount of test automation to reduce regression risk.

B. Automate all the tests for that feature and add them to the automated regression test suite.

C. The changes should be manually tested now and later added to the automation test suit.

D. Do the impact analysis to find out all of the manual and automated tests impacted by this change to meet the new acceptance criteria.

Question 21

"Test automation is important to manage regression risk in Agile projects"

Which TWO of the following reasons support the above statement?

i. To eliminate regression risk due to high code churn

ii. To ensures that all previous iterations' stories are tested.

iii. To receive immediate feedback on overall product quality.

iv. So the team can make changes to previously delivered features to meet the customer's needs.

v. It gives the team more time to spend on the current iteration activities.

Answer:

A. i and ii

B. iv and v

C. iii and iv

D. ii and v

Question 22

Why is test automation a more necessary skill on Agile projects for Testers than on traditional projects?

Select TWO reasons from below.

i.   Features can change in future iterations. Automated tests are necessary to reduce the regression risk due to rapid changes.

ii.   All feature validation testing should be done in the same iteration. In practice, that can only be realized by automated tests.

iii.   Regression testing is a parallel process occurring throughout the iteration. This can only be achieved by automating the tests.

iv.   All tests for the Iteration are required to be finished in the iteration. This is not possible without Automation tests.

v.   Agile testing rely more on white box testing than black box testing.

Answer:

A.   i & ii

B.   ii & v

C.   iv & v

D.   i and iii

Question 23

Which of the following is NOT a typical task performed by the tester on an Agile project?

Answer:

A.   Ensuring proper use of testing tools

B.   Measuring and reporting test coverage.

C.   To maintain the Agile task board for the team.

D.   Configure and manage the test environment and the test data.

Question 24

Which one of the following is a test related organization risk that Agile organizations may encounter?

Answer:

A. Testers work so closely to developers that they lose the appropriate tester mindset

B. Testers managing the test environment and the test data.

C. Testers providing feedback on process quality.

D. Testers helping the team on non-testing activities.

Question 25

The term "Agile task board" relates to which of the following?

Answer:

A. A chart showing the progress of each user story with their current status.

B. A chart showing the sum of estimates of the work delivered across iterations

C. A chart showing the number of defects discovered during a given period

D. A chart showing the amount of work left to be done, versus the time allocated for the iteration

Question 26

Which of the following statements about Test Driven Development (TDD) is FALSE?

Answer:

A.   The TDD process starts with a developer adding a test that captures the concept of a desired function of a small piece of code.

B.   In TDD, developers write the code and run the test in a tight loop until the test passes.

C.   TDD allows the developer to collaborate with other stakeholders, including testers, to define accurate unit tests focused on business needs.

D.   In TDD, developers refactor the code after the test is passed, re-running the test to ensure it continues to pass against the refactored code.

Question 27

Before beginning the first iteration of a project the team is discussing the test strategy for automation. Which of the following is true with respect to Test Pyramid?

Answer:

A.   The team should aim to automate most of the unit/component tests during the sprints.

B.   The team should aim to automate most of the usability tests during the sprints.

C.   The team should aim to automate most of the exploratory tests during the sprints.

D.   The team should aim to automate most of the user story tests during the sprints.

Question 28

The concept of the Test Pyramid is based on which of the following testing principles?

Answer:

A.   Early Testing.

B.   Defect clusters

C.   Pesticide paradox

D.   Exhaustive testing is impossible

Question 29

Which TWO of the following statements demonstrate effective use of the testing quadrants?

1.   The testing quadrants model, and its variants, helps to ensure that all important test types and test levels are included in the development lifecycle

2.   The tester can use the types of tests described in the testing quadrants as a coverage metric, the more tests covered from each quadrant, the higher the test coverage.

3.   The testing quadrants model provides a way to differentiate and describe the types of tests to all stakeholders, including developers, testers, and business representatives.

4.   Testing quadrants are used for risk analysis; with the lower level quadrants representing lower risk to the customer.

5.   Testing quadrants can be used to find out whether the story acceptance criteria is testable.

Answer:

A.   1 and 4

B.   2 and 3

C.   2 and 4

D.   1 and 3

Question 30

Review the Agile team descriptions followed by organization and behavioural practices and then answer the question.

1. Team A: The team has agreed upon a Test process during the Release planning session but the testers are not following it for some of the testing activities in order to finish all stories included in the sprints.

2. Team B: The testers actively participate in all daily stand-up and planning meetings but they are not invited for the retrospective meeting happening at the end of each iteration.

3. Team C: The testers are reporting the testing progress to their Test Manager but the team is not using an Agile task board for monitoring the development and testing tasks

4. Team D: The testers are new to the Agile methodology and they are not able to keep up with the changes during each iterations.

I.   Transparent

II. Open to Feedback

III. Resilience

IV. Credible

Match the teams with the organizational and behavioural practices they are lacking?

Answer:

A. 1-iii, 2-ii, 3-i, 4-iv

B. 1-iii, 2-ii, 3-i, 4-iv

C. 1-iv, 2-i, 3-ii, 4-iii

D. 1-iv, 2-ii, 3-i, 4-iii

Question 31

An Agile team is doing the quality risk analysis for the following user stories selected from the backlog items during an iteration planning session. Match the stories with their respective quality risk based on the information below:

User Story 1: A program to calculate account interest information for the financial end of year report .

User Story 2: A program to display search results in less than 3 secs .

User Story 3: A program to work on different operating systems.

Answer:

A. User Story 1 : Security ,User Story 2: Functional ,User Story 3: Recoverability

B. User Story 1 : Security, User Story 2: performance, User Story 3: Compatibility

C. User Story 1 : Functional, User Story 2: performance, User Story 3: Compatibility

D. User Story 1 : Functional, User Story 2: performance, User Story 3: Recoverability

Question 32

One of the Agile Teams is doing the estimation for the following user story:

"As an online Shopper, I want to delete items from my shopping cart so that I don't purchase items that I decide I don't want"

The tester has asked the following questions to the product owner to get a better understanding of the functionality for estimation purposes. Which of the tester's questions is **not** relevant for the estimation process?

Answer:

A. Tester: "What business benefit does this story deliver?"

B. Tester: "What is the worst thing that could happen with this feature?"

C. Tester: "How will the end user actually use this feature?"

D. Tester: "What is the business priority for this user story?"

Question 33

An agile team is building a new system, to replace a legacy system, to efficiently store customer information using a new relational database. For the testing of this new system, which of the following would best provide relevant information to support testing activities In addition to the user stories?

i. Experience on testing the legacy system.

ii. Performance metrics from the legacy system.

iii. Architecture diagrams of the legacy system.

iv. Customer profiles from the legacy system.

v. Defects list from the legacy system.

Answer:

A. i, iii, iv, v

B. i, ii, iii, v

C. i, iv, v

D. All of the above

Question 34

Which TWO of the following are examples of testable acceptance criteria for test related activities?

Answer:

A. Unit test: All unit tests are Automated

B. Integration test: All major interfaces between the units are tested.

C. System test: All user personas are tested.

D. Security test: The application is vulnerable to external security threats.

E. Recoverability test: The system is able to recover in case of any hardware failure.

Question 35

Review the following User Story for searching for a health care provider on the health insurance website:

"As a customer, I can find a health care provider based on the Region, Category, or suburb information"

Which of the following can be considered as relevant acceptance test cases?

i.   The search window should display within reasonable time.

ii.   Select the Region from the dropdown and click the Search button

iii. Select the Category from the dropdown and click the Search button

iv.   Select the suburb from the dropdown and click the Search button

v.   Select the Region, category and suburb from the dropdown and click the Search button

vi.   Select the health care provider type and click the search button.

Answer:

A.   i, ii, iv

B.   ii, iii, iv

C.   ii, iv, vi

D.   iii, iv, vi

Question 36

Given the following user story:

"An application for the parcel post service calculates the postage rate for parcels up to 10 kg based on the following criteria:

- Standard postage rate for weight under 1 kg
- The postage rate is $20 for weight more than 1 kg and under 2 kg
- The postage rate is flat $35 for weight more than 5 kg

Which of the following is the best black box test design technique for the user story?

Answer:

A. Boundary Value Analysis

B. Decision tables

C. State Transition testing

D. Use Case Testing

Question 37

The Test Manager has organized a meeting with the test team to explore the possibility of exploratory testing after the final iteration for one of the Agile teams. He has shared the following suggestion with the testers. Which TWO of your manager's conclusions are NOT correct?

i.   The Independent test team with be engaged in the testing of user stories. There will be a fixed time to complete the exploratory testing and there is no need to document tests or test results.

ii. Testers will do the risk analysis and will plan the tests of critical things that can go wrong or the potential problem that will make people unhappy.

iii. Business representatives will be used for exploratory testing. They will use the system like the customer would on a day-to-day basis. Testers can help them prioritize and log the defects.

iv. A experienced tester will be used for exploratory testing. Tests should make sure that functionality is correct and to include negative testing. Documentation is not necessary, but defects need to be logged in the defect tracking tool.

Answer:

A.   i & ii

B.   ii & iv

C.   iii & iv

D.   i & iii

Question 38

A new agile team wants to use their single server to build multiple testing and development environments. Which of the following can be used for this purpose?

Answer:

A. Mind maps

B. ALM

C. Electronic task boards

D. Virtualization tools

Question 39

An Agile team wants to build and share an online knowledge base on various aspects of the project. Which of the following tools will be best for that purpose?

Answer:

A. Continuous Integration (CI) tool

B. Wiki

C. ALM

D. Configuration management(CM) tool

Question 40

A Session based test management method is used for which of the following types of testing?

Answer:

A. Acceptance testing

B. System testing

C. Exploratory testing

D. Integration Testing.

Correct Answers and cognitive levels

1	A	K1		21	B	K2
2	C	K1		22	D	K2
3	C,D	K2		23	C	K2
4	D	K2		24	A	K2
5	C	K2		25	A	K1
6	D	K2		26	C	K1
7	C	K1		27	A	K1
8	D	K1		28	A	K2
9	D	K3		29	D	K2
10	B	K2		30	D	K3
11	D	K2		31	C	K3
12	C	K1		32	D	K3
13	D	K1		33	A	K3
14	A	K2		34	A,C	K2
15	C	K2		35	B	K3
16	A	K2		36	A	K3
17	D	K2		37	D	K3
18	D	K2		38	D	K1
19	A	K2		39	B	K1
20	D	K2		40	C	K1

7. Agile Tester Extension Sample Exam 3 - Answer Sheet

Question 1

FA-1.1.1 (K1) Recall the basic concept of Agile software development based on the Agile Manifesto

Justification:

A. Correct – False - The Manifesto consists of 4 key values: Individuals and Interactions over processes and tools; Working software over comprehensive documentation; Customer collaboration over contract negotiation; Responding to change over following a plan

B. Incorrect – True – see (A) for correct answer

C. Incorrect – True – see (A) for correct answer

D. Incorrect – True – see (A) for correct answer

Question 2

FA-1.1.1 (K1) Recall the basic concept of Agile software development based on the Agile Manifesto

Justification:

A. Incorrect – see (C) for correct answer

B. Incorrect – see (C) for correct answer

C. Correct – Collaborating directly with the customer improves the likelihood of understanding exactly what the customer requires and likely to bring more success to the project.

D. Incorrect – see (C) for correct answer

Question 3

FA-1.1.2 (K2) Understand the advantages of the whole-team approach

Justification:

A.   Incorrect – False - the team work together to create user stories.

B.   Incorrect – False - this depends on the skillset of the team; developers may take on this task of non functional testing.

C.   Correct – True - Testers collaborate with the team on all tasks.

D.   Correct –True - quality is everyone's responsibility and all team members should work together to ensure that the desired quality levels are achieved.

E.   Incorrect – False - the team collaborate to prioritize and estimate the user stories.

Question 4

FA-1.1.2 (K2) Understand the advantages of the whole-team approach

Justification:

A.   Incorrect – This is consistent with Agile's whole team approach, testers work in collaboration with product owner and developers for user story creation.

B.   Incorrect – This is consistent with Agile's whole team approach, the product owner can help the testers with testing tasks.

C.   Incorrect –This is consistent with Agile's whole team approach, testers work on non-testing task based on their skillsets.

D.   Correct –This is not consistent with Agile's whole team approach, testers should be part of all discussions.

Question 5

FA-1.1.3 (K2) Understand the benefits of early and frequent feedback

Justification:

A.   Incorrect.

B.   Incorrect.

C.   Correct - See details below

D.   Incorrect

1.   False - early feedback results in consistent project momentum.

2.   True - clarifying customer feature requests and making them available to the customer early will produce a better product and reflect what the customer wants.

3.   False - early feedback can result in more changes and thus more testing.

4.   True - early and frequent feedback results in quality issues found early.

Question 6

FA-1.1.3 (K2) Understand the benefits of early and frequent feedback

Justification:

A.   Incorrect – This task is not related to receiving early and frequent feedback.

B.   Incorrect – This task is not related to receiving early and frequent feedback.

C.   Incorrect –This task is not related to receiving early and frequent feedback.

D.   Correct – As the customer checks the product early and regularly there is less chance for requirement misunderstandings which is the main benefit of early and frequent feedback.

Question 7

FA-1.2.1 (K1) Recall Agile software development approaches

Justification:

A.   Incorrect – See (C) for correct answer.

B.   Incorrect – See (C) for correct answer

C.   correct – Pair programming, test first programming are primary practices for XP backlog, sprints are the instruments & practices for scrum. work-in progress limit, lead time are the instruments for kanban

D.   Incorrect – See (C) for correct answer

Question 8

FA-1.2.1 (K1) Recall Agile software development approaches

Justification:

A.   Incorrect – Scrum Master is a role defined in Scrum. It is the Scrum Master's responsibility to ensure that Scrum practices and rules are implemented and followed, and to resolve any violations, resource issues, or other impediments that could prevent the team from following the practices and rules.

B.   Incorrect – Product Owner is a role defined in Scrum. The Product Owner represents the customer and generates, maintains, and prioritizes the product backlog.

C.   Incorrect – The Development Team is responsible for developing and testing the product. The team is self-organized and is cross-functional.

D.   Correct – There is no separate role defined for the Testing team. The development team cover both developer and tester roles and are responsible for development and testing of the product.

Question 9

FA-1.2.2 (K3) Write testable user stories in collaboration with developers and business representatives

Justification:

A. Incorrect – This is important to the discussion. The tester contributes by ensuring the user story has all non-functional, requirements details.

B. Incorrect – This is important to the discussion. The tester contributes by ensuring the team creates acceptance criteria for the user story.

C. Incorrect –This adds value to the discussion. It is the responsibility of the tester to ask all questions about the missing functionality which may result in the complexities of the product being discussed which the team did not think about earlier.

D. Correct – This is not adding any value to the discussion as the quality characteristics are prioritized by the product owner.

Question 10

FA-1.2.3 (K2) Understand how retrospectives can be used as a mechanism for process improvement in Agile projects

Justification:

A. Incorrect – This should be raised as a process improvement.

B. Correct – The retrospective meeting is not meant to point fingers at individuals or groups.

C. Incorrect –This should be raised as a process improvement.

D. Incorrect – This should be raised as a process problem and bottleneck.

Question 11

FA-1.2.4 (K2) Understand the use and purpose of continuous integration

A. Incorrect

B. Incorrect

C.   Incorrect

D. Correct– see below for detailed justification.

1. Incorrect –Continuous integration reduces repetitive manual testing activities.

2. Incorrect – Continuous integration reduces the regression risk associated with developer code refactoring due to the rapid re-testing of the code base after each small set of changes.

3. Correct – This is a risk for the Continuous integration process.

4. Correct – This is a risk for the Continuous integration process.

Question 12

FA-1.2.5 (K1) Know the differences between iteration and release planning, and how a tester adds value to each activity

Justification:

A. Incorrect – This is expected during release planning.

B. Incorrect – This is expected during release planning.

C. Correct – This is expected during iteration planning.

D. Incorrect – This is expected during release planning.

Question 13

Agile Extension-Term (K1)

Justification:

A. Incorrect – See (D) for correct answer.

B. Incorrect – See (D) for correct answer.

C. Incorrect – See (D) for correct answer.

D. Correct – In an Agile environment, user stories are written to capture requirements from the perspectives of developers, testers, and business representatives. The collaborative authorship of the user story can use techniques such as brainstorming and mind mapping.

Question 14

FA-2.1.1 (K2) Describe the differences between testing activities in Agile projects and non-Agile projects

Justification:

A. Correct –The bugs which creep from previous iterations are a form of Technical debt. Hardening or stabilization iterations occur periodically to resolve technical debt in Agile development.

B. Incorrect – The purpose of hardening or stabilization iterations is not for customer testing.

C. Incorrect – The purpose of hardening or stabilization iterations is not to catch up on automation tasks.

D. Incorrect – Process improvement activities happen in parallel with iteration activities.

Question 15

FA-2.1.2 (K2) Describe how development and testing activities are integrated in Agile projects

Justification:

A. Incorrect

B. Incorrect

C. Correct – see below for detailed justification.

D. Incorrect

i. This is not true, features should be verified in the same iteration in which they are developed

ii. This is required in an Agile project as part of feature validation testing.

iii. This is required in an Agile project as part of regression testing which is a parallel process throughout the iteration.

iv. This is not required in an Agile project. Test level entry and exit criteria are more closely associated with sequential lifecycle models.

Question 16

FA-2.1.3 (K2) Describe the role of independent testing in Agile projects

Justification:

A. Correct – On-demand testers working on final days of each sprint can provide an objective, unbiased evaluation of the software.

B. Incorrect –Testers working on the test strategy is not an example of an independent test team as a lot of collaboration is required with the team for this task.

C. Incorrect – Testers working on iteration automation activities is not an example of an independent test team as a lot of collaboration is required with the team for this task.

D. Incorrect – Testers working on user stories is not an example of an independent test team as a lot of collaboration is required with the team for this task.

Question 17

FA-2.1.3 (K2) Describe the role of independent testing in Agile projects

Justification:

A.   Incorrect – An Independent testing team can work on the test levels like system integration testing that might not fit well within a sprint.

B.   Incorrect – An Independent testing team can work on test data creation which is an iteration-independent activity.

C.   Incorrect – An Independent testing team can work on non functional testing which is an iteration-independent activity.

D.   Correct – User story acceptance testing involves working closely with developers and other team members so there is a chance to lose test independence.

Question 18

FA-2.2.1 (K2) Describe the tools and techniques used to communicate the status of testing in an Agile project, including test progress and product quality

Justification:

A.   Incorrect – See (D) for correct answer

B.   Incorrect – See (D) for correct answer

C.   Incorrect – See (D) for correct answer

D.   Correct – see justification below

1.   Wiki dashboards can be used to automatically generate status reports based on test results and task progress.

2.   In Daily Stand-up meeting issues are communicated so the whole team is aware of the issues and can resolve them accordingly.

3.   Customer satisfaction surveys are used to receive feedback on whether the product meets the customer's expectation (overall product quality).

4.   Agile Task boards are used for instant visual representations of the whole team's current status.

Question 19

FA-2.2.1 (K2) Describe the tools and techniques used to communicate the status of testing in an Agile project, including test progress and product quality

Justification:

A. Correct – Y axis displays the remaining effort which is 8*3=24 & X axis displays the working days

B. Incorrect - See(A) for correct answer

C. Incorrect - See(A) for correct answer

D. Incorrect - See(A) for correct answer

Question 20

FA-2.2.2 (K2) Describe the process of evolving tests across multiple iterations and explain why test automation is important to manage regression risk in Agile projects

Justification:

A. Incorrect – A review of the changes are required first before making any decision. It is unknown if additional automation is required.

B. Incorrect – A review of the changes are required first before making any decision.

C. Incorrect – A review of the changes are required first before making any decision since the tester would not know what new tests would be required for these changes.

D. Correct – This is the initial task to be performed before a decision about any other changes can be made.

Question 21

FA-2.2.2 (K2) Describe the process of evolving tests across multiple iterations, and explain why test automation is important to manage regression risk in Agile projects

Justification:

A. Incorrect.

B. Correct - see below for detailed justification

C. Incorrect.

D. Incorrect.

i. False - Automation can reduce the regression risk but cannot guarantee to eliminate all regression risk.

ii. False - It is not be feasible to automate all of the tests and it is also not possible to retest/rerun all of the test cases from all of the previous iteration.

iii. False - Automated acceptance test results can provide feedback on product quality with respect to the regression since the last build, but they do not provide status of overall product quality.

iv. True - Automation reduces the regression test effort so the team can accept and make changes to previously delivered features to meet the customer's needs.

v. True - Automation reduces the regression test effort so the team can work on tasks from the current iteration

Question 22

FA-2.3.1 (K2) Understand the skills (people, domain, and testing) of a tester in an Agile team

Justification:

A. Incorrect – see justification below.

B. Incorrect – see justification below.

C. Incorrect – see justification below.

D. Correct – see justification below

i. Correct – True - automated tests are required to keep up with frequent changes.

ii. Incorrect – False - feature validation tests are mostly manually.

iii. Correct– True - This involves re-running the automated unit and feature verification tests from the current and previous iterations, usually via a continuous integration framework

iv. Incorrect – False - Automation acceptance tests are not used to finish all the testing during the current iteration they primary use is to make sure the functionality is not impacted due to new changes in the following iterations.

v. Incorrect – False - Neither Automation or Manual testing is more important than the other in Agile projects.

Question 23

FA-2.3.2 (K2) Understand the role of a tester within an Agile team

Justification:

A. Incorrect – True - This activity is expected of the agile tester.

B. Incorrect – True - This activity is expected of the agile tester.

C. Correct – False - Tester is only responsible to maintain **testing tasks** on the Agile task board. Each member of Agile team is responsible to maintain their respective tasks on the Agile task board

D. Incorrect – True - This activity is expected of the agile tester.

Question 24

FA-2.3.2 (K2) Understand the role of a tester within an Agile team

Justification:

A. Correct – True - Agile organizations may encounter this test related risk.

B. Incorrect – This is not a test related organization risk. This is required from an agile tester.

C. Incorrect – This is not a test related organization risk. This is required from an agile tester.

D. Incorrect – This is not a test related organization risk. This is required from an agile tester.

Question 25

Agile Extension-Term (K1)

Justification:

A. Correct – Agile task boards are used to provide an instant, detailed visual representation of the user stories and the whole team's current status.

B. Incorrect – This is a velocity chart, not the Agile task board

C. Incorrect – This is a defect discover rate chart, not the Agile task board

D. Incorrect -This is a burndown chart, not the the Agile task board

Question 26

FA-3.1.1 (K1) Recall the concepts of test-driven development, acceptance test-driven development and behavior-driven development

Justification:

A. Incorrect – This is true of Test-Driven Development (TDD).

B. Incorrect – This is true of Test-Driven Development (TDD).

C. Correct – This is true of behaviour-driven development, not Test-Driven Development.

D. Incorrect – This is true of Test-Driven Development (TDD).

Question 27

FA-3.1.2 (K1) Recall the concepts of the test pyramid

Justification:

A. Correct – The test pyramid emphasizes having more tests at the lower levels and a decreasing number of tests at the higher levels

B. Incorrect – see (A) for correct answer

C. Incorrect – see (A) for correct answer

D. Incorrect – see (A) for correct answer

Question 28

FA-3.1.2 (K1) Recall the concepts of the test pyramid

Justification:

A. Correct – The test pyramid is based on the testing principle of early testing and eliminating defects as early as possible in the lifecycle.

B. Incorrect – The Test pyramid is not related to defect clustering.

C. Incorrect – The Test pyramid is not related to Pesticide paradox.

D. Incorrect – The Test pyramid is not related to Exhaustive testing.

Question 29

FA-3.1.3 (K2) Summarize the testing quadrants and their relationships with testing levels and testing types

Justification:

A. Incorrect

B. Incorrect

C. Incorrect

D. Correct– see justification below.

1. Correct – The testing quadrants can be used to ensure that all test types and test levels are covered.

2. Incorrect – The testing quadrants cannot be used as metrics since not all test levels/types are applicable for system under test.

3. Correct – The testing quadrants can be used as an aid to describe the types of tests and their purpose to all stakeholders.

4. Incorrect – The testing quadrants have no correlation with risk level.

5. Incorrect - Testing quadrants are not related to story acceptance criteria testability.

Question 30

FA-3.1.4 (K3) For a given Agile project, practice the role of a tester in a Scrum team

Justification:

A. Incorrect – see justification below

B. Incorrect – see justification below

C. Incorrect – see justification below

D. Correct – see justification below

1. Testers in Team A are missing credibility.

2. Team B is not open to feedback as the testers are not participating in the retrospectives.

3. Team C is not transparent as the progress of activities are not shared with the team.

4. Team D is not resilient as testers are not able to respond to changes.

Question 31

FA-3.2.1 (K3) Assess product quality risks within an Agile project Justification:

A.   Incorrect- see justification below

B.   Incorrect - see justification below

C.   Correct - see justification below

D.   Incorrect - see justification below

User Story 1: Incorrect calculation(accuracy) in report is a functional risk

User Story 2: Storing customer sensitive information is a performance risk

User Story 3: working on different operating system is Compatibility risk

Question 32

FA-3.2.2 (K3) Estimate testing effort based on iteration content and product quality risks

Justification:

A.   Incorrect – This is relevant. This will help in deciding the business problem this story is solving which will result in a better testing effort estimation.

B.   Incorrect – This is relevant. This will help in deciding the risk and the effort of testing required to cover the risk.

C.   Incorrect – This is relevant. This will help in deciding the testing effort and can be useful for the estimation.

D.   Correct – This is not relevant. Business priority of the user story will not help in estimating the user story.

Question 33

FA-3.3.1 (K3) Interpret relevant information to support testing activities

Justification:

A. Correct – see below

B. Incorrect – see below

C. Incorrect – see below.

D. Incorrect – see below

i. This is helpful to understand the application and to write E2E test cases.

ii. This is not helpful because as a new relational database is being introduced, baselines should be obtained with similar technology or defined performance requirements for this type of technology.

iii. This is helpful to understand the application and to write test cases.

iv. This is helpful to write test cases.

v. This is helpful during the risk analysis phase.

Question 34

FA-3.3.2 (K2) Explain to business stakeholders how to define testable acceptance criteria

Justification:

A. Correct – This is a testable acceptance criteria.

B. Incorrect –This is not testable. It needs to be specific which interfaces are major.

C. Correct – This is testable. A user persona describes a representative (but fictional) individual having specific details (e.g. age 25, married, car owner) that accurately reflect and highlight important features of the user group. User personas are created after the analysis of the user profiles.

D. Incorrect –This is not testable. It needs to specify the details of the external security threats.

E. Incorrect –This is not testable. It needs to specify the time and other recovery parameters.

Question 35

FA-3.3.3 (K3) Given a user story, write acceptance test-driven development test cases

Justification:

A.   Incorrect – see justification below.

B.   Correct – see justification below.

C.   Incorrect – see justification below.

D.   Incorrect – see justification below.

i.   Incorrect – The user story does not mention performance requirements.

ii.   Correct – This test is specific to the search service provider function.

iii.   Correct – This test is specific to the search service provider function.

iv.   Correct- This test is specific to the search service provider function.

v.   Incorrect – The user story is specific to search based on either Region, Category, or suburb information. The question is specific to Either/OR not Any/All

vi.   Incorrect- The user story is specific to the search based on the Region, Category, or suburb information.

Question 36

FA-3.3.4 (K3) For both functional and non-functional behavior, write test cases using black box test design techniques based on given user stories

Justification:

A.   Correct – Boundary Value Analysis(BVA) will be the best option for this story as the testing involves verifying postage rate at boundary values.

B.   Incorrect – A decision table testing is best used to test system which produce different results based on the combinations of inputs.

C.   Incorrect – State Transition testing is best used to test system where outputs are triggered by changes to the 'state' of the system.

D.   Incorrect – Use case testing is best when testing every transaction, of the whole system, from start to finish.

Question 37

FA-3.3.5 (K3) Perform exploratory testing to support the testing of an Agile project

Justification:

A. Incorrect – see justification below.

B. Incorrect – see justification below.

C. Incorrect – see justification below.

D. Correct – see justification below

i. This is not correct – Independent testers are not suitable for exploratory testing.

ii. This is correct – This is true for exploratory testing.

iii. This is not correct– This is an example for user acceptance testing, not exploratory testing.

iv. This is correct – This is true for exploratory testing.

Question 38

FA-3.4.1 (K1) Recall different tools available to testers according to their purpose and to activities in agile projects

Justification:

A. Incorrect – Mind maps can be used to quickly design and define tests for a new feature.

B. Incorrect – An ALM tool can be used to provide visibility into the current state of the application, especially with distributed teams.

C. Incorrect – Electronic task boards are used to manage and track user stories, tests, and other tasks throughout each sprint.

D. Correct – Virtualization tools allow a single physical server to operate as many separate, smaller resources which can be used for development and testing purposes.

Question 39

FA-3.4.1 (K1) Recall different tools available to testers according to their purpose and to activities in agile projects

Justification:

A. Incorrect – A Continuous Integration (CI) tool provides quick response about the build quality and details about code changes.

B. Correct- A Wiki allows teams to build a knowledge base on tools and techniques for development and testing activities

C. Incorrect – An ALM tool provides visibility into the current state of the application, especially with distributed teams.

D. Incorrect –A Configuration management (CM) tool is suitable for providing traceability between versions of software and the tests used

Question 40

Agile Extension-Term (K1)

Justification:

A. Incorrect - see (C) for correct answer.

B. Incorrect – see (C) for correct answer.

C. Correct – A Session based test management method is used for Exploratory testing.

D. Incorrect – see (C) for correct answer.

www.ingramcontent.com/pod-product-compliance
Lightning Source LLC
Chambersburg PA
CBHW071136050326
40690CB00008B/1481